Nonbook Materials

The Organization of Integrated Collections

First edition

Jean Riddle Weihs

Shirley Lewis

Janet Macdonald

in consultation with the CLA/ALA/AECT/EMAC/CAML
Advisory Committee on the Cataloguing of Nonbook Materials

Canadian Library Association, 1973

Published by the Canadian Library Association
151 Sparks Street, Ottawa, Ontario K1P 5E3
Copyright © 1973
Canadian Library Association
ISBN 0-88802-091-0
Printed and bound in Canada

Table of Contents

Joint Advisory Committee on Nonbook Materials

Dr. Margaret Chisholm, Chairman

American Library Association representatives:

Katharine W. Clugston,
Head, Audiovisual Section,
Descriptive Cataloging Division,
Library of Congress.

David G. Remington,
Director of Library Services,
Bro Dart, Inc.,
Chairman, Audio-visual Materials in Libraries
Committee (*ad hoc*) CCS/RTSD/ALA.

Virginia Taylor,
Materials Specialist, Audiovisual,
Instructional Materials Services,
Houston Independent School District.

**Association for Educational Communications
and Technology representatives:**

Margaret Chisholm,
Dean, School of Library and Information
Services,
University of Maryland.

William J. Quinly,
Director, Media Center,
Florida State University.

Alma Tillin,
Technical Services Librarian,
Library Center,
Berkeley (California) Unified School District.

Canadian Library Association representatives:

J. McRee Elrod,
Head, Catalogue Divisions,
University of British Columbia Library.

Lynn Jarman,
Music Cataloguer,
National Library of Canada, Ottawa.
(also represents the Canadian Association of
Music Libraries)

Nancy J. Williamson,
Assistant Professor,
Faculty of Library Science,
University of Toronto.

**Educational Media Association of Canada
representative:**

C. F. Johnston,
Associate Professor of Educational Technology,
Faculty of Education,
Queen's University, Kingston.

The authors of Nonbook Materials: The Organization of Integrated Collections

Shirley Lewis,
Director of Library Services,
Co-operative Book Centre of Canada, Ltd.

Janet Macdonald,
Head, Audio-Visual Department,
North York Public Library.

Jean Riddle Weihs,
Course Director, Library Techniques,
Seneca College of Applied Arts and
Technology.

Foreword

Many segments of society are recognizing that access to information is a vital and fundamental contemporary need. To provide optimum access it is essential to be able to retrieve information in whatever physical format it is found. Such retrieval requires the development of cataloguing codes that will handle all media, including diverse kinds of audio and visual materials. To be most effective these cataloguing guidelines should be acceptable on an international level and should have the support of professional organizations most concerned with these problems.

The Joint Advisory Committee was formed for the purpose of working co-operatively with the authors of this cataloguing manual to represent many organizations concerned with media. The Committee members served as technical consultants, acted in a liaison capacity to keep their organizations informed, transmitted information to the authors, exchanged ideas and view points and served to represent the needs of the users. All of these processes were considered essential in making the manual most representative of the needs of numerous kinds of libraries and media centres and to reflect the philosophies and biases of members of many professional organizations. Also, the committee was particularly concerned with exploring the points of view and approaches to cataloguing represented by theoreticians, conventional bibliographers and people actually concerned with the use of materials in various environments.

The spirit and intent of the committee was to work as constructively as possible to resolve differences of opinion and view points, and to develop a product as acceptable internationally as was possible.

This must be looked upon as a pioneering venture in international co-operation. Many obstacles and differences have been overcome, yet the field of audio and visual media is a new and emerging field. As such, it is undergoing exponential growth and constant change. So we must look on this product as only a beginning and one that must expect to undergo continuing revision as the field grows, matures and stabilizes.

The committee members were dedicated to the task and had a strong sense of a mission to be accomplished. To achieve co-operation in such a complex undertaking is challenging, yet we all recognize that these kinds of tasks cannot be accomplished without it. That statement holds true not only for the present undertaking, but for every step forward in this field in the future.

Committee members fervently hope that this will be the beginning of many future co-operative ventures involving professional organizations at the international level. This process must continue to flourish until the essential tasks are accomplished and total access to information is available for all people in all geographic areas.

Dr. Margaret Chisholm
Chairman of the Joint Advisory Committee
Dean, School of Library and
Information Services
University of Maryland

Introduction

Public service must be the first consideration of a resource centre. The catalogue should be as easy and convenient for the patron to use as is possible without sacrificing the effectiveness of information retrieval. Many patrons, through ignorance or lack of time, are unable to look through several files in different places. Indeed, many are unaware that they have a choice of media in their subject field. Their confusion is compounded when each of these files is governed by its own set of rules. The public is best served when entries for all the media in the collection are interfiled in one omnimedia catalogue, a catalogue in which all circulating and reference materials are entered, described and indexed by the same cataloguing principles.

Nonbook Materials: the Organization of Integrated Collections has been written for all types of libraries and media centres which wish to have an omnimedia catalogue, i.e., one in which the entries for all materials, both book and nonbook, are interfiled. In order to integrate all entries successfully the same cataloguing principles should apply to all media. It is possible to devise a new cataloguing code with, for example, title entry for all materials. This would necessitate the recataloguing of a major portion of existing book collections. A more practical solution is to enter and describe nonbook materials according to the rules already prescribed for books. Therefore, *Nonbook Materials* has developed its rules according to the precepts of Parts I and II of the *Anglo-American Cataloging Rules*, varying these rules only when the nature of the material demands it.

It is impossible to predict new media which may be developed in the future. These rules have been written to encompass the cataloguing of new formats of existing media without the confusion and time lapse which attends the adoption of new rules.

This book presupposes a knowledge of book cataloguing and basic cataloguing principles. Throughout its text, references are made to the *Anglo-American Cataloging Rules*, which is to be used for the detailed construction of main and added entries, dates, format of notes, etc.

Archival collections or those which consist of only one medium may have special cataloguing requirements. If so, the rules in this book can be adapted to suit the particular needs of the collection.

Throughout the book, references are made to card catalogues. The sample cards are laid out in standard 3 x 5 inch format for consistency. However, the cataloguing principles may be utilized in any format and are compatible with machine readable cataloguing concepts from which book or on-line catalogues are constructed.

Computerized cataloguing is dependent upon the same principles as any system of bibliographic control and description. Once the philosophy is established, the program is designed according to the amount of information required in the printout or on the display console. Therefore, the contents of this book are applicable to all catalogue production methods.

Intershelving of all materials by classification number is advocated in the section on storage. It should be noted, however, that the catalogue should be integrated even if the shelving of materials is not.

The preliminary edition of this work was recommended by the Canadian Library Association Council and the American Library Association, Resources and Technical Services Division, Cataloging and Classification Section Executive Committee "as an interim guide for the cataloguing of nonbook materials, with the proviso that a permanent ALA/CLA committee be established to work on any necessary revision for the final edition and its supplements." In fulfilment of this proviso a Joint Advisory Committee on Nonbook Materials was set up to advise the authors of *Nonbook Materials* on the present work. Page iii shows the composition of this Committee, chaired by Dr. Margaret Chisholm. The Committee assisted in the development of terminology, provided helpful suggestions, and read and commented on the drafts of this book. In summer 1972 the Australian School Library Association "formally adopted the standards . . . for use in all schools throughout Australia."

Agreement on terminology is always difficult; concurrence among several groups appears to be even more so. The terms defined here are continuing attempts to create a consistent glossary for cataloguing purposes. If certain terms continue to be troublesome, changes can be made in future editions. The Joint Advisory Committee on Nonbook Materials agreed to the list of media designations found on page 7 and the glossary on pages 87-88. These terms were reviewed by Dr. Donald P. Ely, Chairman of the Committee on Definition and Terminology of the Association for Educational Communications and Technology and liaison to the Steering Group on Educational Technology, Council of Europe and the Internationales Zentralinstitut für das Jugend- Und Bildungs-fernsehen, Munich, publishers of the *Glossary on Educational Technology*. The Library of Congress has accepted this list with two exceptions: audiorecord and microform. The footnote on page 7 gives a brief discussion of the status of the term "audiorecord." The Library of Congress will catalogue microforms as books according to the *Anglo-American Cataloging Rules* (see page 74, paragraph 3).

In the introduction to the preliminary edition comments were requested. The magnitude of the response undoubtedly reflected the need for nonbook cataloguing standards. Letters came from Canada, almost all states of the United States, Great Britain, Australia, and South America. The majority of these letters were from librarians and media specialists in educational libraries ranging from elementary schools to universities, and from teachers of library science. Several were written by public librarians. The only special librarians who responded were those employed by academic libraries. These letters have been of inestimable value, and all the opinions expressed have been taken into consideration in the writing of this book. The authors have consulted producers and users of various media, as well as cataloguers.

In addition to this input, much additional research has been done, particularly in the field of Machine Readable Data Files, Maps, Microforms, Videorecords, and Storage. The authors have attended meetings of the American Library Association, Resources and Technical Services Division, Cataloging and Classification Section's Descriptive Cataloging Committee and Committee on Audiovisual Materials in Librarries, the Canadian Library Association, Technical Services Section's meetings, the Association for Educational Communications and Technology, Information Systems Division's meetings on cataloguing, and a meeting of the Association of Canadian Map Libraries.

Appendix A (page 97-98) has been written in response to requests from map librarians and cataloguing teachers for guidelines for the organization of special map collections. Many correspondents expressed dissatisfaction with both the rules for maps in the preliminary edition of *Nonbook Materials* and in the *Anglo-American Cataloging Rules*. A completely satisfactory method of map cataloguing has not yet been formulated. This book presents the cataloguer with a choice of three systems: the *Anglo-American Cataloging Rules*, the rules on page 49-52, or rules in Appendix A. The first two methods will allow map entries to be filed in an integrated catalogue; the last will make such interfiling much more complex.

Comments about this work are invited and should be addressed to Mrs. Jean Weihs, c/o Canadian Library Association, 151 Sparks St., Ottawa, Canada K1P 5E3. Such correspondence is much appreciated and will provide valuable input for the future editions of this work.

Acknowledgements

It is impossible to detail the many contributions made by individuals and organizations to this work. We are indebted to the Joint Advisory Committee on Nonbook Materials and its chairman, Dr. Margaret Chisholm, for encouragement, information, and constructive criticism. We wish to thank the Association for Educational Communications and Technology, the American Library Association, the Canadian Library Association, and the Educational Media Association of Canada for the support they gave their representatives to the Joint Advisory Committee. They encouraged librarians and audiovisual specialists from Canada and the United States to work co-operatively in the hope that a beginning could be made toward the international standardization of nonbook cataloguing rules.

Harry Weihs spent many weary hours re-reading and editing the final manuscript. David Nevin, Chief, Audiovisual Department and Photo-duplication Lab., Washington University Libraries answered every inquiry and prompted officials of concerned organizations to write to us. Special tribute must be given to the Canadian School Library Association Technical Services Committee, and its chairman, Mrs. Helen Donaldson. Their original recognition of the need for integration of nonbook cataloguing, and their enthusiasm, provided the necessary impetus that has led to the present edition. Work on the preliminary edition was completed in consultation with the committee, as follows: Reverend W. Brown, Mrs. V. Doan, Mrs. H. Donaldson, Mrs. D. Fennell, Miss A. Guignard, Mrs. J. Henderson, Sister P. Leightizer, Mrs. S. Lewis, Miss J. Macdonald, Mr. D. Pettem, Miss M. Scott, Mrs. J. Riddle Weihs, Miss M. Weston. Assistance was also given on the preliminary edition by the following consultants: Mrs. C. Bilsland, Mr. M. Campbell, Miss F. Fowler, Mrs. E. Hoy, Mrs. C. Morin, Miss N. Williamson. Although the Canadian School Library Association Technical Services Committee is now disbanded, many of the former members sent very helpful suggestions during the writing of the present volume.

Douglas Pettem, Coordinator of Library Services, Borough of North York Board of Education, responded quickly to frequent requests for help. School librarians and media specialists from many parts of Metropolitan Toronto were equally enthusiastic. We appreciated their help.

The following organizations made their staff and resources available for our research: Canadian Book Wholesale Ltd., Encyclopaedia Britannica (Canada), Bellevue-Pathe Systems Ltd., University of Toronto Department of Zoology, University of Toronto Media Centre, Scarborough Public Library, Canadian Broadcasting Corporation, Ontario Educational Communications Authority.

We were fortunate in receiving help from professional organizations. Four committees of the American Library Association, Resources and Technical Services Division Cataloging and Classification Section allowed us to use materials from their discussions: the Descriptive Cataloging Committee, the Subcommittee on Machine Readable Data Files, the Audio-Visual Materials in Libraries Committee, and the Subject Analysis and Organization of Library Materials Committee. The Library Association Media Cataloguing Rules Committee (Great Britain) also shared their deliberations with us. Information was received from the National Microfilm Association and from several members of the Association of Canadian Map Libraries. The Canadian Library Association, Technical Services Division, Committee on the Revision of the *Anglo-American Cataloging Rules*, and particularly its chairman Dr. Ronald Hagler, gave this work substantial support.

The support of our employers, Seneca College of Applied Arts and Technology, the Co-operative Book Centre of Canada Ltd., and the North York Public Library was greatly appreciated.

Jean Riddle Weihs
Shirley Lewis
Janet Macdonald

Cataloguing Policy for Nonbook Materials 1

Cataloguing Policy for Established Libraries

In order to establish their book cataloguing procedures, all libraries must make certain policy decisions. These will include:

- a classification scheme;
- the depth of classification within the scheme;
- a book numbering system, such as Cutter numbers or call letters;
- a subject heading system;
- the extent and detail of descriptive cataloguing and added entries.

As a library evolves into a media centre, its cataloguing policies should include similar decisions covering all media. An integrated omnimedia catalogue must be governed by a set of rules which applies to all items listed therein. Therefore, the media centre may elect to modify its book cataloguing to fit new procedures developed for its nonbook items or to extend its existing cataloguing policies to all media. Since the former decision would necessitate recataloguing, the latter procedure appears to be the wiser one.

It must be emphasized that the subject analysis systems chosen by a library for its book collection should be used for all media.

Cataloguing Policy for New Media Centres

A new media centre which has no previously formulated cataloguing policy should consider the following points in determining its cataloguing procedures.

1. External bibliographic aids

Commercial and centralized cataloguing services and other sources of cataloguing information will use standardized rules. These are likely to be consistent for all book and nonbook materials.

2. Classification or accession number for information retrieval

The use of the same classification scheme for all media centre materials is suggested for the following reasons:

a) media centre patrons will find it easier to become acquainted with and to use one system;

b) wherever possible, materials on the same subject will be stored together;

c) emphasis is placed on content rather than form;

d) centralized cataloguing and processing services will not assign non-standardized call numbers, e.g., accession numbers.

Classifying materials for integrated collections necessitates flexible storage and the use of trained personnel. This would not be the case if materials were to be organized by accession number. Nevertheless, storage by accession number is not recommended for the following reasons:

a) materials on the same subject would not be housed together because there is no relationship between call number and subject matter;

b) added copies of a particular item may have different call numbers and be stored in different places;

c) the only subject approach to materials would be through the catalogue;

d) call numbers must be assigned by individual resource centres, thereby diminishing the economy of centralized cataloguing services.

3. Classification schemes

The media specialist should choose a classification scheme which is comprehensive, continuously revised, and proven in day-to-day use. The selection of a particular scheme is based generally on the anticipated size of the collection and the degree of specificity required in classification. The schemes used most commonly by certain types of libraries are listed below. No attempt has been made to evaluate the advantages and disadvantages of the various schemes.

Many academic and research libraries are using the Library of Congress classification or the unabridged Dewey Decimal classification. Special libraries devoted to specific disciplines may use subject oriented classification schemes, e.g., National Library of Medicine classification for health science collections. The Bibliographic Systems Center, School of Library Science, Case Western Reserve University (The Sears Library Building, Cleveland, Ohio 44106) provides information on various classification systems, current research, and future trends.

Public libraries and many secondary school media centres report the use of the unabridged Dewey Decimal classification to the second and third prime marks, depending on the anticipated size of the collection. Libraries with small collections use the abridged Dewey, but keep in mind their plans for expansion and the possibility of future incorporation into a larger system.

Juvenile collections in elementary school media centres and public libraries are for the most part classified by the abridged Dewey Decimal classification, although the unabridged Dewey has been used successfully at this level.

Collections, which are not organized for browsing, may be shelved by some other scheme. However, the assignment of a classification number, at the time the material is in the cataloguing department, may prove to be of future benefit should shelving policy change or catalogue computerization be undertaken. Many media centres with computers have enjoyed the benefit of being able to use a classification scheme to produce subject bibliographies and lists.

4. Call letters, author or book numbers

The decision whether to use call letters or specific numbering systems, e.g., Cutter numbers, will depend generally on the size of the collection. Three call letters are usually sufficient to identify a particular item in a school media centre or a small-to-medium public library collection. Larger collections prefer the use of specific book or author numbers to assign a unique call number to each item.

5. Measurement

Consideration should be given to the use of metric measurements in the collation and notes in view of the international trend toward the adoption of the metric system. Media for which metric concepts are not pertinent, e.g., videotapes, should be described in inches.

6. Subject headings

Preference should be given to a subject heading system which is comprehensive and periodically revised. The same subject heading system should be used for book and nonbook materials. The systems used most commonly by certain types of media centres are listed below. No attempt has been made to evaluate the advantages and disadvantages of the various systems.

Library of Congress subject headings are used in many academic, research, and special libraries. Special libraries devoted to specific disciplines may use subject-oriented, authoritative, up-dated lists, e.g., MeSH headings for health science collections. Where in-depth indexing is required, the principles of thesaurus construction are applied.

Library of Congress subject headings are used also in large adult collections in many public libraries and secondary school media centres. Most centres with small collections report the use of Sears subject headings. However, those with large growth potential tend to use Library of Congress headings even though their collection may remain small for a few years.

Juvenile collections in public libraries and elementary school media centres generally use Sears subject headings. However, there is a trend toward Library of Congress subject headings especially modified for juvenile literature, which have been endorsed as the national standard by the Executive Committee of the Resources and Technical Services Division, American Library Association on the recommendation of the Cataloging of Children's Materials Committee. Many of these headings have been incorporated into the 10th edition of *Sears List of Subject Headings*.

7. Media form subdivisions for subject headings

Media form subdivisions should not be used in an omnimedia catalogue. Headings are assigned on the basis of subject content only; format is disregarded in subject headings. Details about a particular item are ascertained by reading the catalogue card, in the same way that a catalogue user determines the specific format of a book from the descriptive cataloguing. Thus the subject cataloguing of books and other media is uniform.

8. Added entries

The purpose of added entries is to enable a catalogue user to find a particular item by some name or title other than the main entry heading. Added entries also group materials in useful ways, e.g., by performer. The number and kind of added entries required will depend on the nature of catalogue use in each media centre. Rule 33 in the *Anglo-American Cataloging Rules* provides detailed instruction concerning added entries.

The Cataloguing of Materials as Individual Items or Sets

Many materials are purchased in sets which can be processed either as collective cataloguing units (series) or as separate items with a series note indicating their relationship.

In the nonbook field, this problem arises particularly with filmstrips, but it is also encountered in other media.

In deciding whether to keep a set together or to break it up and catalogue each item separately, the cataloguer must consider the type of materials, the media centre, and the needs of the user. Subject analysis often affects the decision. If each unit within a set would have significantly different classification numbers and subject headings, it may be advantageous to catalogue each part of the set separately. If, on the other hand, each unit within a set would have the same classification and subject headings, it is probably more efficient to catalogue the series as a unit.

Sample card 1

```
341.13      United Nations today series    (Filmstrip)   McGraw-Hill, c1964.
UNI            6 rolls. col.

            Teacher's guide (6 p.)
            Contents.-   1. History of the United Nations (39 fr.)-  2. Organ-
            ization of the United Nations (36 fr.)-  3. The United Nations family
            of agencies (35 fr.)-  4. The United Nations and the end of colonial-
            ism (35 fr.)-  5. Achievements and problems of the United Nations
            (35 fr.)-  6. A day at the United Nations (34 fr.)


            1.  United Nations.   2.  International cooperation.
```

Set catalogued
as a unit

Sample card 2

```
301.329711
BRI         British Columbia population patterns  (Filmstrip)  National Film
               Board of Canada, c1968.
               35 fr. col.  (Geography of British Columbia series)

            Manual  (8 p.)




            1. British Columbia - Population   I. Series.
```

Set catalogued
by each
component #1

Sample card 3

```
551.409711
BRI         British Columbia landforms  (Filmstrip)  National Film Board of
            Canada, c1968.
            41 fr.  col.  (Geography of British Columbia series)

            Manual  (8 p.)




            1. Landforms - British Columbia.   I. Series.
```

Set catalogued
by each
component #2

Methods of Indicating Type of Medium

A. Colour-coding

The use of white rather than colour-coded catalogue cards is recommended for the following reasons.

1. Uniformity of colour emphasizes the multimedia approach to resource centre materials.
2. New methods of catalogue reproduction make colour-coding impractical because:
   a) colour-coding is not used in book catalogues;
   b) the cost of colour film for photocopying catalogue cards is prohibitive.
3. Centralized cataloguing services use white cards. Individual resource centres using such services and desiring colour-coded cards would have to colour-code by hand, a time-consuming task. To make colour-coding economically feasible in centralized cataloguing, an internationally accepted standardized colour code would have to be established. At present there is no such standardization.
4. As new types of media are acquired, the media centre would soon run out of distinctive colours. Shadings of colours could lead to confusion if the quality of colour on the card stock were not maintained.

B. Media code

The use of a media code is not recommended. A media code used as an integral part of the call number proved to be unsatisfactory in field tests. This type of call number resulted in individual items being stored by medium, and the segregated shelving thus destroyed the concept of an integrated multi-media collection. In addition, the intershelving of items within a particular medium resulted in an uneconomic use of space, since many media are produced in widely divergent sizes. A wiser use was made of storage space when the media code was abandoned and all media were intershelved. Oversized materials were then treated in the same manner as oversized books.

A media code does not identify a medium as well as the more accurate media designations (*see* below). Since a media code is not an effective agent for storage or medium identification, its use as an integral part of the call number should be discouraged.

If their size permits intershelving, all items should be stored by one classification scheme. Any item which can be housed with other media does not need an additional notation on the catalogue card. Each media centre must fashion its own method of indicating unusual storage.

If an item cannot be intershelved in its proper place in the classification scheme, its location should be stated on the catalogue card in accordance with the method adopted for reference and oversized books.

C. Media designations

The generic designation, given in parenthesis following the title, will be amplified if necessary in the collation and notes.

The medium designation is given early on the card to inform the user succinctly and immediately about the type of material listed. Users interested in this type of material will be prepared to read further for more detail. Users not interested in this general type of material may move on to the next listing.

The generic term is used to avoid the proliferation of media designations which may develop if specific designations are used. It is anticipated that the list of media designations shown below will be hospitable to future media. In addition, generic media designations will allow a resource centre to produce a basic card which, exclusive of collation, can be used for works reproduced in various formats of the same medium (*see* sample card 23).

The media designations are:

Audiorecord[1] – includes sound recordings of all types, cylinder, disc, roll, tape, wire
Chart – includes flip chart, wall chart
Diorama
Filmstrip – includes filmslip
Flash card
Game
Globe
Kit (two or more media which are not fully interdependent and, therefore, may be used separately)
Machine readable data file – includes computer datacell, disc, drum, magnetic tape, paper tape, punched card, etc.

Map – includes relief map
Microform – includes aperture card, microfilm, microfiche, micro-opaque
Microscope slide
Model – includes mock-up
Motion picture – includes kinescope recording, motion picture loop
Picture – includes art original, art print, photograph, post card, poster, study print
Realia (consists of specimens, samples, artifacts)
Slide – includes stereograph
Transparency
Videorecord – includes videocassette, videodisc, videotape, electronic video recording, etc.

Laboratory kits and programmed learning will be catalogued under the medium designation which best describes the item.

Definitions of the media included in the above designations are given in the glossary on pages 87-88.

Collation and notes for each medium will be found with the discussion of that medium.

Media centres which have used more specific designations need not recatalogue, but may switch to the generic terms for new material.

Specific terms may be necessary in a specialized collection, such as an art centre. It is advisable, however, for such a centre to keep its list of designations as generic as possible.

---

[1] The term "audiorecord" has been selected for use in this work on the advice of the Joint Advisory Committee on Nonbook Materials. The use of this term is tentative at the present time (October 1972) pending a decision by the parties which control the revision of the *Anglo-American Cataloging Rules*: the American Library Association, the Canadian Library Association, the Library Association (Great Britain), and the Library of Congress. Other terms are being considered; for example, the Library of Congress has proposed the term "recording." When a decision has been made, the authors will announce it in appropriate library journals.

General Information Concerning Sample Cards

Except where indicated in the margin beside the sample cards, the 18th unabridged edition of the *Dewey Decimal Classification, Subject Headings used in the Dictionary Catalogs of the Library of Congress*, and *A List of Canadian Subject Headings* have been used as examples. Subject analysis systems used in an established library for a book collection should be applied to all media.

One card format has been used throughout the book for consistency. There is no standard format used by all centres. The format used in cataloguing the resource centre's book collection should be used for all media.

Sample cards 4, 5 and 6 illustrate some of the subject analysis systems, call numbers, and descriptive cataloguing detail which may be used by different media centres. The cataloguing in sample card 4 is used only in instances where the needs of the users are unsophisticated and where a small media centre staff makes detailed cataloguing impractical. It must be emphasized that the same cataloguing policy should be applied to all resource centre materials.

Commercial cataloguers are likely to provide a standard of cataloguing which will appeal to the largest market. Detailed cataloguing may be supplied since it is easier to delete or ignore the items on the card which are not useful than to add items which are needed.

The sample cards for filmstrips demonstrate common cataloguing principles which should be applied to all nonbook materials. These principles are noted at the right-hand side of the card.

917.13　City in transition: metropolitan Toronto　(Kit)　Ottawa, Dept. of
CIT　　　Energy, Mines and Resources, Geographical Branch and NFB,
　　　　[1970?]
　　　　1 book, 1 filmstrip, 8 maps, 30 slides, 4 study print sets,
　　4 transparencies.

　　　　Manuals.

　　　　1. Metropolitan areas.　2. Toronto metropolitan area.

Suggested simplified cataloguing for juvenile collections – abridged Dewey Decimal classification, call letters, Sears subject headings and limited descriptive cataloguing.

Sample card 5

<pre>
917.13541 City in transition: metropolitan Toronto (Kit) Ottawa, Dept. of
C498   Energy, Mines and Resources, Geographical Branch. Made by
                National Film Board of Canada [1970?]
                1 book, 1 filmstrip, 8 maps, 30 slides, 4 study print sets,
            4 transparencies.

                Manuals.
                Book titled: The changing face of Toronto, by D. Kerr and
            J. Spelt. Ottawa, Queen's Printer, 1965.

                1. Cities and towns - Planning - Toronto.   2. Toronto - Description.
            3. Toronto - Maps.   4. Toronto metropolitan area.   I. Kerr, Donald
            Gordon Grady. The   changing face of Toronto.   II. Title:
            The changing face of   Toronto.
</pre>

Suggested cataloguing for adult collections in public libraries and secondary school media centres – unabridged Dewey Decimal classification, Cutter number or call letters, Library of Congress subject headings, and some notes.

Sample card 6

<pre>
NA   City in transition: metropolitan Toronto (Kit) Ottawa, Dept. of
9130   Energy, Mines and Resources, Geographical Branch, c1956-70.
T7   Made by National Film Board of Canada [1970?]
C58   1 book, 1 filmstrip, 8 maps, 30 slides, 4 study print sets,
1970   4 transparencies.

              Manuals.
              Map symbol sheet, slides and transparencies text, and some
          maps in French and English.
              Each transparency has overlays attached.
              Book titled: The changing face of Toronto; a study in urban
          geography, by Donald Kerr and Jacob Spelt. Ottawa, Queen's

                                              (Continued on next card)
</pre>

Suggested detailed cataloguing for academic and research libraries – Library of Congress classification and subject headings, detailed descriptive cataloguing.

Sample card 6
(continued)

<pre>
NA   City in transition: metropolitan Toronto (Kit) [1970?] (Card 2)
9130
T7
C58   Printer, 1965. (Canada. Geographical Branch. Memoir, II)
1970

              1. Cities and towns - Planning - Toronto.   2. Toronto - Description.
          3. Toronto - Maps.   4. Toronto metropolitan area. I. Canada.
          Geographical Branch.   II. National Film Board of Canada.   a.a. Kerr,
          Donald Gordon Grady.
</pre>

Cataloguing Rules for Nonbook Materials

General Rules for Entry and Descriptive Cataloguing

The general rules below apply to all nonbook materials. Exceptions to these rules are dictated by the nature of a particular medium and will be discussed under the medium heading.

All items must be examined by the cataloguer and should be screened or played to ensure accuracy of bibliographic information.

Main entry

If a media centre wishes to have an integrated catalogue in which all media, book and nonbook, are interfiled, the same rules of entry must apply to all materials.

Entry under title will occur more frequently for nonbook materials because authorship cannot be established as readily for many nonbook items.

The following rules of main entry are to be applied in the order in which they are listed. Detailed instructions for formulating main entry will be found in Part I of the *Anglo-American Cataloging Rules.*

1. A reproduction of a work originally produced in another medium is entered in the same manner as the original work.
2. A work for which authorship can be clearly established is entered under author.[1] Authorship is not normally attributed to consultants, performers, producers, directors, designers, etc.
3. A work for which author entry is inappropriate because of the extent and nature of collaborative authorship is entered under title.

Title

The multiplicity of titles on some audiovisual works necessitates an order of precedence for establishing the correct title.

The source of the title should be the following, in the order listed:

1. The material itself, including the container when it is an integral part (e.g., a cassette) or the unifying part (e.g., the box of a kit or game) of an item. If there is more than one title on the material, precedence is given to the one positioned closest to the physical content.
2. Accompanying data, e.g., manuals, sheets, etc., issued with the item.
3. The container, where it is not an integral or unifying part of the item (*see* 1 above) and, therefore, may be discarded.

4. Other sources. If the above sources do not provide adequate information, the title may be taken from whatever available source is considered the most reliable, and enclosed in square brackets.
5. If no title can be found, the cataloguer will supply one and enclose it in square brackets.

Medium designation

The type of medium being catalogued is always shown in the singular in parenthesis immediately following the title statement. *See* page 7 for the list of media designations.

Additional information in the body of the card

Statements of authorship, illustration, edition, etc., will be listed after the medium designation in the form and order prescribed in Part II of the *Anglo-American Cataloging Rules.*

Performance, production, and other credits are given in the form in which they are listed on the item. Such credits may be included in the body of the card or in a note. In general, credits which are particularly significant and can be stated briefly are listed in the body of the card. Lengthy or less significant credits are recorded in a note (*see* sample cards 58, 90, 91, 92, etc.).

Imprint

Elements of the imprint:

1. *Place.* Place need not be given unless this information will help locate obscure producers or distinguish between two producers with similar names. Place is generally given for government printing offices if this cannot be ascertained by reading the catalogue card.
2. *Producer or manufacturer.* The rules for citing publisher in Part II of the *Anglo-American Cataloging Rules* are followed. A producer or manufacturer who has a commonly used acronym or shortened form of name, e.g., NFBC for National Film Board of Canada, or SVE for Society for Visual Education, may be given in this form if it will be understood by the media centre's public.

---

[1] The *Anglo-American Cataloging Rules* defines author as "the person or corporate body chiefly responsible for the creation of the intellectual or artistic content of a work. Thus composers, artists, photographers, etc., are the 'authors' of the works they create."

3. *Distributor and releasing agent.* The names of these organizations are recorded if significant.
4. *Date.* Preference is given first to the latest date shown on the material itself, and secondly to the latest date on accompanying materials, such as manuals. If these materials are undated, outside sources are searched. If no date can be found, the cataloguer supplies one in accordance with the rules for uncertain dates in the *Anglo-American Cataloging Rules.* Dates derived from outside sources are enclosed in square brackets.

Collation

The following is a general list of collation components. Physical characteristics necessary for the description of any particular medium are included in the discussion of that medium.

Number of pieces. The number and type of format in the unit being catalogued is listed, e.g., 1 chart, ½ disc or ½ audiodisc, 4 pictures. A media centre may elect to use the term "various pieces" if the nature of a many-piece set is not deemed important enough to account for every piece (*see* sample cards 57-59, etc.).

Qualifier. If the medium designation is not specific enough to identify the format precisely, a qualifier is listed in the collation, e.g., the qualifier "tape" in sample cards 25, 115, etc.

Colour. Colour is given if applicable. The following terms are used, in combination with each other when appropriate: col., b&w, sepia, tinted.

Sound. Sound or silent is given if applicable. The following abbreviations are used: sd., si.

Size. The size of two-dimensional media is given height x width, that of three-dimensional media height x width x depth. Size may be taken to the nearest centimetre or inch.

Duration. Playing or running time is given to the nearest minute. Total playing time of less than one minute is given in seconds. This information is always included when readily available. If a decision is made to include playing time in all cases, it will be necessary for the cataloguer to play many items.

Playing time of the complete unit being catalogued is listed in the collation; playing time for any part thereof is given in the notes.

Accompanying media. If a set of two or more interdependent media has been catalogued by the dominant medium, the less significant media are listed in alphabetical order at the end of the collation before the series statement. This listing may be as brief or as detailed as desired by the individual media centre (*see* sample cards 19, 20).

Series statement. If applicable, a series statement in parenthesis follows the physical description. When an item is part of two series, both are listed at the end of the collation, each enclosed in its own parenthesis. The more specific series is listed first, the more general last (*see* sample card 115).

Notes

Notes are essential to emphasize special and/or unusual features of the material, e.g., manuals, teaching guides, special equipment. Contents notes are desirable for many items. Part II of the *Anglo-American Cataloging Rules* provides detailed guidelines for the construction of notes.

The number of pages in accompanying material is noted in parenthesis after the word describing such material, e.g., Manual (16 p.). Some manuals, handbooks, or guides are promotional in nature and have limited value. These need not be listed on the catalogue card.

The suggested order for notes is:
1. Supplementary collation information.
2. Accompanying materials.
3. Information supplementing elements in the formalized description.
4. Persons or organizations involved in the performance or production of the work.
5. Relationship to other works.
6. Other notes.
7. Contents.

Summaries

Summaries are not necessary for media which can be readily examined or adequately described by title and/or series statement. However such items as motion pictures or videorecords usually require description in a summary.

A summary should describe subject content succinctly and objectively without evaluation.

If clarity can be maintained, words and phrases may be substituted for sentences.

Tracing

See page 4 for a discussion of subject headings and added entries.

Audience level

The inclusion of audience level is a matter of local preference, since such information may not be desirable in a public catalogue, particularly for juvenile and youth collections.

Since there is no general agreement concerning a list of terms for audience level, the following list[1] is recommended as sufficient for most users: Preschool; Primary; Elementary; Secondary; Adult; General; Specialized (for specialized audiences, e.g., doctors, social workers, librarians).

---

[1] Extracted from U.S. Library of Congress. MARC Development Office. *Films, a MARC format . . . ,* Washington, 1970.

Audiorecords

Audiorecord: a recording of sound.

Cylinders, discs, rolls, wires, and tapes (open reel-to-reel, cartridge, and cassette) are included under this heading and designated by the term Audiorecord.

The general rules on pages 13 to 14 apply, with the additions and exceptions noted below. Media centres requiring more detail in cataloguing music are referred to the *Anglo-American Cataloging Rules*, Chapters 13, 14.

Main Entry

1. The work(s) of one composer or author are entered under the name of that composer or author. (*See* sample cards 9-11, 14-22)
*2. The work(s) of more than one composer or author issued with a collective title are entered under that title. (*See* sample cards 12-13, 26, 28, 30, 32, 34)
*3. The works of more than one composer or author issued without a collective title require separate entries for each work. These entries are always linked together by a "With" note. (*See* section under **Notes** below and sample card 24)

Uniform title

The use of a uniform title is necessary to bring together various versions and arrangements of musical compositions. (*See* sample cards 9, 14-15, 17, 21-22, 24, and non-musical work sample card 18)

Uniform titles for musical works are formulated according to the rules outlined in the *Anglo-American Cataloging Rules*, Chapter 13.

If the uniform title is not immediately available, a line is left between the main entry heading and the title on the audiorecord so that the uniform title can be added later. (*See* sample card 16)

Medium designation[1]

The medium designation follows the uniform title for musical works. (*See* sample cards 9, 14-15, 17, 21-22, 24) In all other cases, the medium designation follows the title of the audiorecord. (*See* sample cards 10-13, 16, 18-20, 25-35)

---

* See page 17 for *Alternative rule* for entry under Performer.
[1] See footnote on page 7.

Imprint

Publisher. The name of the publisher is followed by the serial identification. Matrix numbers are used only if they are the only serial identification on the material. (*See* sample card 12)

Date of release is given in the imprint. Date of performance is given in a note. (*See* sample card 22)

Collation

Physical description is given in the following order:

DISCS
Number of discs or portions of discs.
Size in inches is given in parenthesis.
Playback speed.
Playing time in minutes, if significant and readily available. (*See* sample cards 20-21)
Recording mode, e.g., monaural, stereo- or quadraphonic, in abbreviated form.

OPEN REEL-TO-REEL TAPES
Number of tapes or portions of tapes. (*See* sample card 24)
Size of reel in inches is given in parenthesis. (*See* sample card 24)
Playback speed.
Playing time in minutes, if significant and readily available.
Recording mode, e.g., monaural, stereo- or quadraphonic, in abbreviated form.

CARTRIDGES AND CASSETTES
Number and type of container or portion of container. (*See* sample cards, 14, 32-33)
Playing time in minutes, if significant and readily available.
Recording mode, e.g., monaural, stereo- or quadraphonic, in abbreviated form.

Notes

Notes are listed in the order given below. Media centres requiring more extensive detail are referred to the *Anglo-American Cataloging Rules*, Chapters 13 and 14.

1. "*With*" note: Where separate entries are necessary for two or more works issued together, the other works are listed in the order in which they appear on the label. The composer/author is given first, inverted and in secondary fullness, followed after a period by the title of the work. This infor-

mation is always given in the form in which it appears in the separate entry. (*See* sample card 24)

2. *Form,* or *species,* e.g., opera in 2 acts, drama, etc., if readily available and not evident from the title. (*See* sample card 32) This note may be combined with the performer note (*see* sample cards 15, 26-29, 32-35) and/or the text note (*see* sample card 11)

3. *Names of performers* and their *medium of performance,* if not otherwise evident. (*See* sample cards 9-10, 14, 16, 21-22, 24-25, 34-35) This note may be combined with the contents note to relate performers to particular works in collections. (*See* sample card 13)

4. *Text.* Notes concerning the language and source of the text, the edition recorded and its relationship to other works are given if readily available. This note may be combined with the performer note. (*See* sample cards 10-11, 18, 20)

5. *Place and date of performance,* if significant and readily available. (*See* sample card 22)

6. *Duration* of individual works, if readily available. (*See* sample card 16) This note may be combined with the contents note. (*See* sample card 22)

7. *Supplementary collation information,* e.g., 8 track, manual sequence, audible advance signals, etc. (*See* sample cards 9, 19-20)

8. *Supplementary visual materials,* e.g., libretti, song sheets, manual, etc. (*See* sample cards 18-20, 30-31)

9. *Contents.* Sample cards 9-10, 13, 18, 22, 26-35 demonstrate various presentations of this information.

Added entries
Title added entries are never made for non-distinctive uniform titles which require the name of the composer for accurate identification, e.g., Quintet, wood-winds & horn, no. 2. (*See also* **References** below)

If the work for which an added entry is made requires a uniform title, the uniform title must be used in the added entry. (*See* sample cards 17, 24B, 25)

References
Because musical works appear under so many variant titles, composer/title *see* references must be made from well-known titles not used to the uniform title used, especially when the uniform title is in a language unfamiliar to the majority of the catalogue users:

Sample card 7

Dukas, Paul Abraham.
   The sorcerer's apprentice

    SEE

Dukas, Paul Abraham.
   L'apprenti sorcier

Title references can take the place of many added entries which would otherwise add unnecessary bulk to the catalogue:

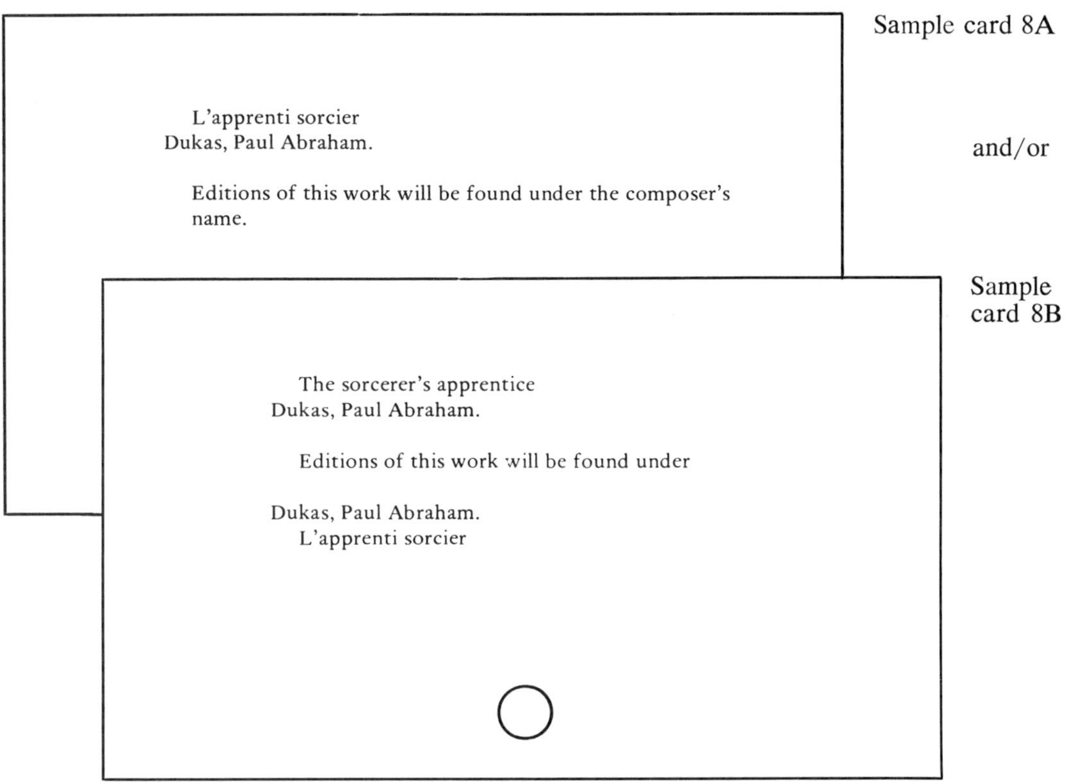

Sample card 8A

and/or

Sample card 8B

Alternative Rule

Entry Under Performer(s)

Collections of works by more than one author or composer, with or without a collective title supplied by the publisher, may be entered under the performer or performing group.

For the purposes of these rules, the term *performer* refers to an individual, the term *performers* refers to a performing group. A performing group is any organization or group of persons that is identified by a name and that performs as an entity.

Performing groups cover a broad range of categories. Some of the more common are instrumental groups, choral groups, dramatic groups. Most musical works require performance by combinations of these groups with each other and/or with individual performers such as soloists and conductors.

Choice of performer(s) to be used as main entry depends on the relative importance of their contribution to the performance, which in turn depends on the nature of the work performed.

Main entry

Enter under the person or group primarily responsible for the artistic interpretation of the works performed. (*See* sample cards 29, 31, 33)

Where responsibility is *equally* shared the following rules apply:

1. Two or more individuals – enter under the first named. (*See* sample card 27)
2. One individual and a group or groups – enter under the individual. (*See* sample cards 25, 35)
3. More than one individual and a group or groups – enter under the first named individual.
4. More than one group – enter under the first named.

Designation of function

The designation *conductor* or *performer(s)* is added to all main entry headings for persons performing these functions. These designations are not used in added entry headings.

All other elements of entry and description are recorded as indicated on the preceding pages, with the following exceptions.

Title and composer/author statement
The title is recorded as it appears on the label, even though it may consist solely of the name(s) of the performer(s). (*See* sample cards 34-35)

Where there is no collective title, the title and composer/author of each work is recorded as it appears on the label. These statements are separated by periods. (*See* sample card 25) Long lists of works more intelligibly presented in a contents note are omitted after the first item. All such omissions are indicated by three dots.

If the label does not express adequately the relationship of the composer/author to the work cited, an explanatory word or phrase in the language of the title is added in square brackets after each title. (*See* sample card 25)

Added entries
Added entries should be made for other performer(s) in accordance with the provisions of the *Anglo-American Cataloging Rules*, Chapters 1 and 14.

Title added entries are not made for titles which consist solely of the name of the performer(s). (*See* sample card 35)

Sample card 9

```
785.1154   Mozart, Johann Chrysostom Wolfgang Amadeus.
MOZ            [Symphonies. Selections]  (Audiorecord)
           The last six symphonies.  Odyssey 32 36 0009  (32 16 0181,
           32 16 0183, 32 16 0023)  [1968]
               3 discs (12 in.)  33 1/3 rpm.  mono.

               Royal Philharmonic orchestra; Sir Thomas Beecham, conductor.
               Manual sequence.
               Contains nos. 35-36 and 38-41  (K. 385, 425, 504, 543, 550
           and 551)

               1. Symphonies - To 1800.   I. Royal Philharmonic Orchestra.
           II. Beecham, Sir Thomas          bart.
```

Entry under composer.

Serial numbers given for each disc.

Performer note.

Supplementary collation note.

Informal contents note.

Sample card 10

```
398.2      Andersen, Hans Christian.
AND            The little match girl, and other tales  (Audiorecord)  Caedmon
           TC 1117.  [196-?]
               1 disc (12 in.)  33 1/3 rpm.  mono.

               Read by Boris Karloff.
               Translated by Reginald Spink from the author's Eventyr.
               Contents.-  The swineherd.-  The top and the ball.-  The red
           shoes.-  Thumbelina.-  The little match girl.

               I. Karloff, Boris.  II. Title.
```

Entry under author.
Performer note.
Source of text.
Contents note.

Sample card 11

```
822      Michaels, Sidney.
MIC          Dylan  (Audiorecord)  Columbia DOS 701  (DS 6591-6593)
         [1964]
             3 discs (12 in.)  33 1/3 rpm.  stereo.

             Drama, starring Alec Guiness, based on Caitlin Thomas' Leftover
         life to kill and John Malcolm Brinnin's Dylan Thomas in America.
             Notes on the play, synopsis, and biographical sketches (20 p.)
         laid in container.

             1. Thomas, Dylan, in fiction, drama, poetry, etc.  I. Guiness,
         Alec.  II. Thomas, Caitlin.  Leftover life to kill.  III. Brinnin, John
         Malcolm.  Dylan          Thomas in America.  IV. Title.
```

Entry under dramatist.

Form, performer, related works notes combined.

Supplementary visuals note.

Added entries for related works.

Sample card 12

```
331.761   Computer careers  (Audiorecord)  Willowdale, Ont., Second
COM           Century A/V [matrix no. T-56251-56256.  1970]
              3 discs (12 in.)  33 1/3 rpm.  mono.  (Canadian career series)




              1. Electronic data processing - Vocational guidance.
              2. Programming (Electronic computers) - Vocational guidance.
```

Entry under title.

Place given in imprint.

Matrix numbers.

Sample card 13

```
785.3052  Music by Arensky, Borodin, Glière, Khachaturian, Liadov &
MUS           Shostakovich  (Audiorecord)  Mercury SR 90346.  [1963]
              1 disc (12 in.)  33 1/3 rpm.  stereo.  (Great music by Russian
          composers)

              "Character pieces, a Russian tradition, by Edward Downes"
          on slipcase.
              Contents.-  Variations on a theme by Tchaikovsky, by Arensky
          (Philharmonia Hungarica; Antal Dorati, conductor)-  Baba-Yaga,
          The enchanted lake, and Kikimora, by Liadov (Eastman Philhar-
          monia; Howard Hanson, conductor)-  Armenian dances, by
          Khachaturian (Eastman Wind Ensemble)-  Overture (London

                             (Continued on next card)
```

Entry under title.

Performer and contents notes combined.

Sample card 13
(continued)

785.3052　Music by Arensky, Borodin, Glière, Khachaturian, Liadov &
MUS　　　　　Shostakovich　(Audiorecord)　Mercury SR 90346.　[1963]
　　　　　　(Card 2)

　　　　　　Symphony Orchestra; Antal Dorati, conductor) and March
　　　　　　(Eastman-Rochester "Pops"; Frederick Fennell, conductor)
　　　　　　from Prince Igor, by Borodin.-　Russian sailors dance, by Glière,
　　　　　　and Polka from The age of gold, by Shostakovich (Eastman-
　　　　　　Rochester "Pops";　Frederick Fennell, conductor)

　　　　　　1. Orchestral music.

Extension card.

Sample card 14

782.8154　Bock, Jerry.
BOC　　　　　[Fiddler on the roof.　Selections]　(Audiorecord)
　　　　　　Music from Fiddler on the roof.　RCA Camden C8S-1036.
　　　　　　[196-?]
　　　　　　　1 tape cartridge.　stereo.

　　　　　　　Living Strings.

　　　　　　　1. Musical revues, comedies, etc. - Excerpts.　I. Living Strings.
　　　　II. Title:　Music from Fiddler on the roof.

Uniform title.
Performer note.

Sample card 15

782.8554　Herman, Jerry.
HER　　　　　[Hello, Dolly.　Selections]　(Audiorecord)
　　　　　　Hello, Dolly!　Original motion picture soundtrack.　Music and
　　　　　lyrics by Jerry Herman.　20th Century Fox Records DTCS-5103.
　　　　　　[1969]
　　　　　　　1 disc (12 in.)　33 1 /3 rpm.　stereo.

　　　　　　　Film musical, starring Barbra Streisand and others, with chorus
　　　　　and orchestra; Lenni Hayton and Lionel Newman, conductors.

　　　　　　　1. Motion-picture music - Excerpts.　I. Streisand, Barbra.
　　　　II. Hayton, Lennie.　III. Newman, Lionel.　IV. Hello, Dolly (Motion
　　　　picture)

Uniform title.

Form and
performer notes
combined.

Added entry for
related work.

<table>
<tr><td>

785.7571
BER

      Berwald, Franz.

          Piano quintet no. 1, in C minor. Piano quintet no. 2, in A major (Audiorecord) Nonesuch Records H 71113. [1966]
          1 disc (12 in.) 33 1/3 rpm. stereo.

          Benthien Quartet; Robert Riefling, piano.
          Duration: 24 min., and 28 min., respectively.

          1. Piano quintets. I. Berwald, Franz. Piano quintet no. 2, in A major. II. Benthien Quartet. III. Riefling, Robert.

</td></tr>
</table>

<table>
<tr><td>

813
MEL

Klise, Thomas S.
   Melville (Audiorecord) Written and narrated by Thomas S.
Klise. Thomas S. Klise Co. 26981-26982. [196-?]
    1 disc (12 in.) 33 1/3 rpm. mono., and 1 filmstrip (The
American imagination)

   Automatic and audible advance signals.
   Reading script (16 p.) with credits and bibliographies.

    1. Melville, Herman. I. Series.

</td><td>

Sample card 19

Audiorecord with
interdependent
accompanying
medium. (Abridged
collation for latter)

Supplementary
collation note.

Supplementary
visuals note.

Series traced.

</td></tr>
</table>

<table>
<tr><td>

818
THO

Thoreau, Henry David
   An interview with Henry David Thoreau (Audiorecord) Edited
by Thomas M. Johnson. Scott, Foresman XCTV 97108-97109.
c1964.
    1 disc (12 in.) 33 1/3 rpm. 30 min., and 1 filmstrip. 111 fr.
col. 35 mm.

   Excerpts from Thoreau's writings read by Hans Conried in answer
to questions of a present-day student.
   Automatic advance signals only. Reading script (8 p.) cued to
photographs of Walden and the Thoreau Memorial at the Hall of
Fame.

    I. Title.

</td><td>

Sample card 20

Audiorecord with
interdependent
accompanying
medium. (Full
collation for latter)

Source of text
and performer
notes combined.

Supplementary
collation and
visuals notes
combined.

</td></tr>
</table>

<table>
<tr><td>

785.7471
BOR

Borodin, Aleksandr Porfir'evich.
   [Quartet, strings, no. 1, A major] (Audiorecord)
   String quartet no. 1, in A major. Westminster W 9015. [1963]
    1 disc (12 in.) 33 1/3 rpm. 30 min. mono.

   Vienna Konzerthaus Quartet.
   Previously issued under serial no.: 18715.
   Programme notes by Peter Hugh Reed on slipcase.

    1. String quartets. I. Konzerthaus-Quartett.

</td><td>

Sample card 21

Uniform title.

Duration in collation.

</td></tr>
</table>

```
782.554    Offenbach, Jacques.
OFF            [Overtures. Selections]  (Audiorecord)
               Famous overtures.  Music Guild MS 814.  [1971]
               1 disc (12 in.)  33 1/3 rpm.  stereo.
               Vienna State Opera Orchestra; Hermann Scherchen, conductor.
               Recorded in Mozart Hall, Vienna, December, 1961; previously
           released as Westminster WST 17035.
                   Contents.-  La vie Parisienne (5 min.)-  Orphee aux enfers (11 min.)
           Monsieur et Madame Denis (7 min.)-  La belle Helene (10 min.)-
           La grande duchesse de Gerolstein (4 min.)-  Barbe-bleue (6 min.)

                   1. Overtures.  I. Scherchen, Hermann.  II. Wiener Staatsoper.
           Orchester.
```

Uniform title
for collection.

Date of per-
formance note.

Duration and
contents notes
combined.

The following card is a Library of Congress sample of a basic card which, exclusive of collation, can be used for works reproduced in various formats of the same medium:


```
Keyboard immortal Sergei Rachmaninoff plays again, in
    stereo.  [Phonorecord.  Sun Valley, Calif.]  Superscope
    [1970]  (The Keyboard immortal series, 1)
       disc A001.  2 s.  12 in.  33⅓ rpm.
       cartridge 2–A001.  8-track.
       cassette 1–A001.  2½ x 4 in.
       reel 3–A001–S.  7 in.  3¾ ips.

    Stereophonic.
    Recorded by the Welte reproducing piano from piano rolls.
    Program notes on slipcase of disc and on reel container.


                            (Continued on next card)
                                                      00–0000
                                                         R
```



```
Keyboard immortal Sergei Rachmaninoff plays again, in
    stereo.  [Phonorecord]  (Card 2)

       CONTENTS.—Prelude in C♯ minor, op. 3, no. 2.  Prelude in G
    minor, op. 23, no. 5.  Étude tableau in B minor, op. 39, no. 4.
    Étude tableau in A minor, op. 39, no. 6.  Elegie in E♭ minor, op.
    3, no. 1.  By Rachmaninoff.—Grande valse brillante in E♭ major,
    op. 18.  Nocturne in F major, op. 15, no. 1.  Scherzo in B♭ minor,
    op. 31.  By Chopin.


       1. Piano music.    I. Rachmaninoff, Sergei, 1873–1943.  Works,
    piano.  Selections.  Phonodisc.  1970.  II. Chopin, Fryderyk Fran-
    ciszek, 1810–1849.  Works, piano.  Selections.  Phonorecord.  1970.

                                                      00–0000
    Library of Congress                                  R
```

The sample cards on the following pages demonstrate the use of the **Alternative Rule** for entry under Performer.

Each collection has been catalogued first according to the rules on pages 15-17, then according to the **Alternative Rule** on pages 17-18.

Sample card 24A

785.3052   Dukas, Paul Abraham.
DUK   [L'apprenti sorcier] (Audiorecord)
         The sorcerer's apprentice. London LCL 80151. [1964]
         1/3 tape (7 in. reel) 7 1/2 ips. stereo.

         With: Ravel, Maurice. La valse, orchestra.- Honegger, Arthur. Pacific 231.
         Orchestre de la Suisse romande; Ernest Ansermet, conductor.

         1. Symphonic poems. I. Orchestre de la Suisse romande. II. Ansermet, Ernest Alexandre.

Separate entries for works issued without collective title.

Portion of tape in collation.

"With" note.

Sample card 24B

785.3052   Ravel, Maurice.
DUK   [La valse, orchestra] (Audiorecord)
         La valse. Bolero. London LCL 80151. [1964]
         1/3 tape (7 in. reel) 7 1/2 ips. stereo.

         With: Dukas, P.A. L'apprenti sorcier.- Honegger, Arthur. Pacific 231.
         Orchestre de la Suisse romande; Ernest Ansermet, conductor.

         1. Boleros (Orchestra) 2. Waltzes (Orchestra) I. Ravel, Maurice. Bolero, orchestra. II. Orchestre de la Suisse romande. III. Ansermet, Ernest Alexandre.

"With" note.

Sample card 24C

785.3052   Honegger, Arthur.
DUK   [Pacific 231] (Audiorecord)
         Pacific 231. London LCL 80151. [1964]
         1/3 tape (7 in. reel) 7 1/2 ips. stereo.

         With: Dukas, P.A. L'apprenti sorcier.- Ravel, Maurice. La valse, orchestra.
         Orchestre de la Suisse romande; Ernest Ansermet, conductor.

         1. Orchestral music. I. Orchestre de la Suisse romande. II. Ansermet, Ernest Alexandre.

"With" note.

785.052   Ansermet, Ernest Alexandre, conductor.
ANS   The sorcerer's apprentice [by] Dukas. La valse [and] Bolero [by] Ravel. Pacific 231 [by] Honegger. (Audiorecord) London LCL 80151. [1964]
      1 tape (7 in. reel) 7 1/2 ips. stereo.

      Orchestre de la Suisse romande; Ernest Ansermet, conductor.

      1. Orchestral music. 2. Boleros (Orchestra) 3. Symphonic poems. 4. Waltzes (Orchestra) I. Dukas, Paul Abraham. L'apprenti sorcier. II. Ravel, Maurice. La valse, orchestra. III. Ravel, Maurice. Bolero, orchestra. IV. Honegger, Arthur. Pacific 231. V. Orchestre de la Suisse romande.

Alternative Rule

Sample card 25

Entry under conductor.

Title/composer statement.

Added entries for individual works in the collection.

784.30622 Country boy and country girl (Audiorecord) RCA Victor LSP
COU   4434. [1970]
      1 disc (12 in.) 33 1/3 rpm. stereo.

      Vocal duets; Jimmy Dean and Dottie West, principally with the Jordanaires and instrumental ensemble.
      Contents.- Slowly.- Jackson.- For the good times.- Let it be me.- Yours love.- Sweet thing.- Put it off until tomorrow.- I got you.- Just someone I used to know.- I wish I didn't have to miss you.

      1. Music, Popular (Songs, etc.) I. Dean, Jimmy. II. West, Dottie. III. Jordanaires.

Sample card 26

Entry under collective title.

Form and performer notes combined.

784.30622 Dean, Jimmy, performer.
DEA   Country boy and country girl (Audiorecord) RCA Victor LSP 4434. [1970]
      1 disc (12 in.) 33 1/3 rpm. stereo.

      Vocal duets; Jimmy Dean and Dottie West, principally with the Jordanaires and instrumental ensemble.
      Contents.- Slowly.- Jackson.- For the good times.- Let it be me.- Yours love.- Sweet thing.- Put it off until tomorrow.- I got you.- Just someone I used to know.- I wish I didn't have to miss you.

      1. Music, Popular (Songs, etc.) I. West, Dottie. II. Jordanaires. III. Title.

Alternative Rule

Sample card 27

Entry under first named performer.

Added entries for other performer(s)

<table>
<tr><td>

784.306
BES

The Best of the Guess Who (Audiorecord) RCA Victor LSPX
1004. [1971]
1 disc (12 in.) 33 1/3 rpm. stereo.

Songs performed by the Guess Who.
Contents.- s. 1. These eyes. Laughing. Undun. No time.
American woman. No sugar tonight/New mother nature.- s. 2.
Hand me down world. Bus rider. Share the land. Do you miss
me darlin'. Hang on to your life.

1. Music, Popular (Songs, etc.) I. Guess Who.

</td><td>

Sample card 28

Entry under
collective title.

Form and per-
former notes
combined.

Contents note.

Added entry for
performers.

</td></tr>
</table>

<table>
<tr><td>

784.306
GUE

Guess Who, performers.
The Best of the Guess Who (Audiorecord) RCA Victor LSPX
1004. [1971]
1 disc (12 in.) 33 1/3 rpm. stereo.

Songs performed by the Guess Who.
Contents.- s. 1. These eyes. Laughing. Undun. No time.
American woman. No sugar tonight/New mother nature.- s. 2. Hand
me down world. Bus rider. Share the land. Do you miss me darlin'.
Hang on to your life.

1. Music, Popular (Songs, etc.) I. Title.

</td><td>

Alternative Rule

Sample card 29

Entry under
performers,

</td></tr>
</table>

Sample card 30

786.4052 Josef Hofmann performs in 1913 (Audiorecord) Recorded
JOS   Treasures 662, 683
   [1963-
     discs (12 in.) 33 1/3 rpm. stereo. (The Welte legacy of
piano treasures)

   "Transfers from the Welte reproducing piano".
   Biographical notes ([5] p.) inserted in slipcase of v. 1.
   Contents.- [v. 1.] Rondo capriccioso, op. 14, E major, by Mendels-
sohn. Variations, D minor, by Handel. Sonata, op. 31, no. 3, E flat,
by Beethoven.- v. 2. Tannhauser overture, by Wagner-Liszt. Feuer-
zauber, by Wagner-Brassin. Polonaise, op. 44, F minor [and] Polonaise
fantasy, op. 61, A major, by Chopin.

   1. Piano music.   2. Piano music, Arranged. I. Title.
II. Series.

Entry under
collective title.

Open entry.

Series.

Supplementary
visuals note.

Series traced.

Alternative Rule

Sample card 31

786.4052 Hofmann, Josef, performer.
HOF   Josef Hofmann performs in 1913 (Audiorecord) Recorded
   Treasures 662, 683
   [1963-
     discs (12 in.) 33 1/3 rpm. stereo. (The Welte legacy of
piano treasures)

   "Transfers from the Welte reproducing piano".
   Biographical notes ([5] p.) inserted in slipcase of v. 1.
   Contents.- [v. 1.] Rondo capriccioso, op. 14, E major, by Mendels-
sohn. Variations, D minor, by Handel. Sonata, op. 31, no. 3, E flat,
by Beethoven.- v. 2. Tannhauser overture, by Wagner-Liszt. Feuer-
zauber, by Wagner-Brassin. Polonaise, op. 44, F minor [and] Polonaise
fantasy, op. 61, A major by Chopin.
   1. Piano music.   2. Piano music, Arranged. I. Title.
II. Series.

Entry under
performer.

<table>
<tr><td>

784.30633   The Mills Brothers' great hits (Audiorecord) Dot DC 25157. 1958.
MIL   1 tape cassette. stereo.

        Songs.
        Contents.- Program 1. Paper doll. Nevertheless. Till then.
Cielito lindo. Lazy river. Rockin' chair.- Program 2. You always
hurt the one you love. Across the alley from the Alamo. I'll be
around. Glow worm. Basin Street blues. Be my life's companion.

        1. Music, Popular (Songs, etc.) I. Mills Brothers.

</td><td>

Sample card 32

Entry under
collective title.

Form note.

Added entry for
performers.

</td></tr>
</table>

<table>
<tr><td>

784.30633 Mills Brothers, performers.
MIL   The Mills Brothers' great hits (Audiorecord) Dot DC 25157. 1958.
         1 tape cassette. stereo.

        Songs.
        Contents.- Program 1. Paper doll. Nevertheless. Till then.
Cielito lindo. Lazy river. Rockin' chair.- Program 2. You always
hurt the one you love. Across the alley from the Alamo. I'll be
around. Glow worm. Basin Street blues. Be my life's companion.

        1. Music, Popular (Songs, etc.) I. Title.

</td><td>

Alternative Rule

Sample card 33

Entry under
performers.

</td></tr>
</table>

<table>
<tr><td>

784.306   Big Brother and the Holding Company (Audiorecord) Columbia
BIG   C 30631. [1971]
         1 disc (12 in.) 33 1/3 rpm. stereo.

        Songs performed by Big Brother and the Holding Company,
featuring Janis Joplin, lead singer.
        Contents.- Bye, bye baby.- Easy rider.- Intruder.- Light is
faster than sound.- Call on me.- Coo-coo.- Women is losers.-
Blindman.- Down on me.- Caterpillar.- All is loneliness.- Last time.

        1. Music, Popular (Songs, etc.) I. Big Brother and the Holding
Company. II. Joplin, Janis.

</td><td>

Sample card 34

Entry under
collective title.

Form and per-
former notes
combined.

Contents note.

</td></tr>
</table>

784.306 Joplin, Janis, performer.
JOP   Big Brother and the Holding Company (Audiorecord) Columbia
C 30631. [1971]
1 disc (12 in.) 33 1 /3 rpm. stereo.

Songs performed by Big Brother and the Holding Company,
featuring Janis Joplin, lead singer.
Contents.- Bye, bye baby.- Easy rider.- Intruder.- Light is
faster than sound.- Call on me.- Coo-coo.- Women is losers.-
Blindman.- Down on me.- Caterpillar.- All is loneliness.- Last time.

1. Music, Popular (Songs, etc.) I. Big Brother and the Holding
Company.

Care, handling, and storage
See page 92 for General Guidelines for the
Care, Handling, and Storage of Magnetic Tape,
and page 91 for the Care, Handling, and
Storage of Audiodiscs.

Charts

Chart: a sheet of information arranged in tabular or graphic form produced on an opaque backing.

Charts and flip charts are included under this heading and designated by the term Chart.

Charts may be organized as ephemeral materials, in a vertical file (*see* pages 81-82). Items of permanent value to the collection should be

completely catalogued for their effective use.

The general rules on pages 13 to 14 apply with the following additions and exceptions.

Collation
Number of charts.
Colour.
Size of the mount in centimetres or inches.

629.1309   History of flight (Chart) Educational Posters, c1959.
HIS   1 chart. col. 38 x 26 in.

1. Aeroplanes - History. 2. Flight - History.

Sample card 36

200.9   Sparks, John B.
SPA   The histomap of religion; the story of man's search for spiritual
         unity (Chart) Rand McNally, c1964.
         1 chart. col. 150 x 70 cm.

1. Religion - History. I. Title.

Sample card 37

Entry under author.

Sample card 38

```
940.27     Napoleon  (Chart)  Hammond, c1968.
NAP            1 chart.  col.  28 x 147 cm.




              1. Napoleon I, Emperor of the French.   2. Europe - Hist. -
           1789-1815.
```

Sample card 39

```
025.3      Bergwall, Charles.
B454v          Vicalog; Eye Gate visual card catalog  (Chart)  Conceived and
           designed by Charles Bergwall and Sherwin S. Glassner.   Eye Gate
           [196-?]
               1 chart.  b&w.  23 x 35 cm.

               1 opaque sheet with 4 transparencies hinged at top.



               1. Catalogs, Card.  2. Cataloging.  I. Glassner, Sherwin S.
           II. Title.
```

Cutter number.

Care, handling, and storage
See General Guidelines for the Care, Handling, and Storage of Two-Dimensional, Opaque Materials on page 93.

Dioramas

Diorama: a scene produced in three dimensions
by placing objects, figures, etc., in front of a
representational background.
   The general rules on pages 13 to 14 apply
with the following additions and exceptions.

Collation
Number of pieces (the use of the term "var-
ious pieces" is optional)
Colour.

Sample card 40

<table>
<tr><td>525.5
SEA</td><td>Seasons - fall and winter   (Diorama)   Instructo Products, c1966.
various pieces.   col.   (Instructo activity kit).

Teacher information sheets.

1. Autumn.   2. Winter.</td></tr>
</table>

Care, handling, and storage
See General Guidelines for the Storage of
Three-Dimensional Media on page 93.

Filmstrips

Filmstrip: a roll of film containing a succession of images designed to be viewed frame by frame, with or without sound. A short length of film, sometimes mounted in rigid format, is called a *filmslip*.

Filmstrips and filmslips are included under this heading and designated by the term Filmstrip.

The general rules on pages 13 to 14 apply with the following additions and exceptions.

Main entry

Preference should be given to the information on the title frames rather than the leader frames. Title frames immediately precede the main body of the filmstrip while the leader frames are separated from the body of the filmstrip by a length of blank film.

Collation

If the item is a filmslip this information is stated first. (*See* sample card 48)

Number of frames. The last numbered frame or, if applicable, the last numbered double frame, is recorded. If the frames are unnumbered, the collation will list 1 roll, 1 filmstrip, or 1 filmslip.

Option no. 1: If a media centre considers information about the number of frames essential, the frames in an unnumbered filmstrip may be counted and this information added in square brackets to the collation, e.g. [48] fr. The count should begin with the first content frame and end with the last content frame, thereby excluding title, credit, and end frames.

Option no. 2: If a media centre wants to list the number of frames, but does not wish to spend time counting frames, it can use the following method which will give a fairly accurate approximation for single frame filmstrips. Measure from the first content frame to the last content frame. There are 16 frames to every foot (12 inches) of filmstrip. e.g. length = 50 inches; no. of frames = 50 x 16/12 = 66.67 which represents 67 frames.

Colour.

Sd. or si. (This information is optional. Media centres which do not have filmstrips with sound tracks may omit this item in the collation.)

Size. Width is recorded in millimetres. (This information is optional. Most filmstrips are 35 mm. and some media centres will wish to indicate millimetre size only if it is other than 35 mm.)

Notes

If the images in a double-frame filmstrip are placed such that a projector with a swivelling device must be used in order to utilize the filmstrip effectively, this information is noted. (*See* sample card 47)

The sample cards for filmstrips demonstrate common cataloguing principles which should be applied to all nonbook materials. These principles are noted on the right of the card.

813   Krauss, Ruth.
KRA   A hole is to dig ... (Filmstrip) Pictures by Maurice Sendak.
Weston Woods [1968]
1 roll. col.

Manual (16 p.)
Reproduction of book published by Harper & Row, 1952.

I. Sendak, Maurice, illus. II. Title.

Sample card 41

Reproduction of book.

<table>
<tr><td>

578.8
VAN

Vance, Adrian G.
    Introduction to stem sectioning and staining (Filmstrip)
Society for Visual Education, 1962.
    1 roll. col. (The Microscope and its use, 4)

    Captions.

    1. Stains and staining (Microscopy) 2. Botany - Technique.
I. Series.

</td><td>

Sample card 42

Entry under author.

</td></tr>
</table>

<table>
<tr><td>

025.3
B454

Bergwall, Charles.
    Introduction to the card catalog (Filmstrip) Written by
Charles Bergwall and Sherwin S. Glassner. Eye Gate, c1962.
    35 fr. col. 35 mm. (Library services)

    Captions.

    1. Catalogs, Card. I. Glassner, Sherwin S. II. Series.

</td><td>

Sample card 43

Cutter number.
Joint authors.

</td></tr>
</table>

<table>
<tr><td>

709.32
FIV

5,000 years of Egyptian art (Filmstrip) Educational Productions,
    c1968.
    28 double fr. col.

    Notes (10 p.) by A.E. Halliwell.

    1. Art, Egyptian.

</td><td>

Sample card 44

Double frame.

</td></tr>
</table>

421.5   Initial consonant sounds   (Filmstrip)   Society for Visual Education,
INI   1959.
            6 rolls.   col.   (Basic primary phonics, group one)

            Contents.-   B,D, and P.-   L,H,F, and K.-   M,N,T, and J.-   R,S,V,
and W.-   C,G,Y, and Q.-   Practice and review.

            1. English language - Consonants.   I. Series.

Sample card 45

Cataloguing of a set.

Contents note.

797.23   An Introduction to snorkel and scuba diving   (Filmstrip)   Fitness
INT   and Amateur Sport Directorate, Dept. of National Health and
            Welfare. Made by National Film Board of Canada, c1966.
            40 fr.   col.

            1. Skin and scuba diving.   I. Canada.   Fitness and Amateur
Sport Directorate.

Sample card 46

More than one
issuing or
sponsoring body.

901.92   Reeves, Marjorie.
REE   The medieval world   (Filmstrip)   Longmans, 1968.
            2 rolls.   double fr.   col.   35 mm.   (Then and there filmstrips)

            Manual (20 p.)
            Images placed in frame horizontally and vertically.
            Correlated with medieval titles in Longmans' Then and there
book series.

            1. Civilization, Medieval.   I. Title.   II. Series.

Sample card 47

Double frame set.

Special equipment
needed.

<table>
<tr><td>821
GRA</td><td>Grasshopper green   (Filmstrip)   Slide & Filmstrip Productions
　　　　[196-?]
2 filmslips.   col.

Teacher's guide (5 p.)

1. Locusts - Poetry.</td></tr>
</table>

Filmslip.

<table>
<tr><td>591.151
GER</td><td>Gering, Robert L.
　　Sex determination and sex linkage   (Filmstrip)   Ward's Natural
Science Establishment, 1971.
　　96 fr.   col., and 1 audiotape cassette (19 min.)   (Ward's solo-
learn system)

　　1. Sex - Cause and determination.   2. Sex-linkage (Genetics)
I . Title.</td></tr>
</table>

Filmstrip with
interdependent
accompanying
medium.

Sample card 50

```
972.91     Cuba:  ten years of Castro   (Filmstrip)   New York times, c1969.
CUB            70 fr.  col., and 1 audiodisc (40 min.)

           Manual (15 p.)




           1. Castro, Fidel.   2. Cuba - Hist. - 1959-
```

Filmstrip with interdependent accompanying medium.

Sample card 51

```
301.31     Felger, Richard.
FEL            The ecological crisis   (Filmstrip)   Cathedral, c1971.
               6 rolls (45 fr. each)  col., and 3 audiodiscs (20 min. each)

           Study guides and scripts included.
           Contents.-  Population statistics.-  Population control.-
           Ecological considerations.-  Evolution and extinction.-  Pesticides.-
           Pollution.



           1. Human ecology.   2. Pollution.   I. Title.
```

Set of filmstrips with interdependent accompanying medium.

Contents note.

Sample card 52

```
629.1309    The History of flight   (Filmstrip)   Teaching Resources Development
HIS             Center, c1970.
                1 roll.   col., and 1/2 audiotape cassette.   (Highlights of history)

                With:  The Printed word   (Filmstrip)




            1. Aeronautics - History.
```

Filmstrip with interdependent accompanying medium.

First filmstrip dependent upon a single audio-tape cassette.

"With" note.

Sample card 53

```
629.1309    The Printed word   (Filmstrip)   Teaching Resources Development
HIS             Center, c1970.
                1 roll.   col., and 1/2 audiotape cassette.   (Highlights of history)

                With:  The History of flight   (Filmstrip)




            1. Printing - History.
```

Filmstrip with interdependent accompanying medium.

Second filmstrip dependent upon a single audio-tape cassette.

"With" note.

Care, handling, and storage

See General Guidelines for the Care, Handling, and Storage of Film Media on page 92.

The rapid development in methods of shelving filmstrips with other media make true intershelving possible. These shelving aids range from containers which simulate book binding to book ends containing filmstrip storage.

Flash Cards

Flash card: a card printed with words, numerals, or pictures, designed for rapid identification, with or without sound.

Flash cards may be organized in a picture file (see pages 81-82). Items of permanent value to the collection should be completely catalogued for their effective use.

The general rules on pages 13 to 14 apply with the following additions and exceptions.

Collation
Number of cards.
Colour.
Size of the mount in centimetres or inches.

Sample card 54

Sample card 55

Entry under author.

Abridged Dewey decimal classification.

Sears subject headings.

Care, handling, and storage
See General Guidelines for the Care, Handling, and Storage of Two-Dimensional, Opaque Materials on page 93.

Games

Game: a boxed set of materials designed for play or competition.

The general rules on pages 13 to 14 apply with the following additions and exceptions.

Collation

Number of pieces (the use of the term "various pieces" is optional).

Colour, if applicable.

Size, if this information is meaningful.

Notes

Notes may be essential to indicate use.

Sample card 56

793.74   Allen, Layman E.
ALL   Equations; the game of creative mathematics (Game) Science Research Associates, c1966.
         32 dice.

         Game board printed on container.
         Player's manual (16 p.)

         1. Mathematical recreations. I. Title.

Sample card 57

HV   Toll, Dove.
4030   Ghetto (Game) Designer: Dove Toll. Developed by Academic
T645   Game Associates. Western Publishing Co., c1969.
         various pieces. (Simu-learn)

         Manual (24 p.) by Dove Toll.
         Summary: 7-10 players are introduced to the emotional physical and social world of the poor.

         1. Poor. I. Academic Games Associates. II. Title.

Sample card 58

```
HD          Creative Studies, inc.
6961            Strike; an educational simulation   (Game)  Macmillan, c1971.
                various pieces.

                Player's manual (18 p.) and teacher's manual (16 p.)
                Credits:  Writer-editors, Stephen J. Fischer and Raymond A.
                Montgomery; research writer, Marcia Kaunfer.
                Summary:  Designed to provide awareness of the complexities
                of labour-management relations.


                1. Industrial relations.  I. Title.
```

Sample card 59

```
330         Market; a simulation game   (Game)  Benefic Press, 1971.
MAR             various pieces.   (Economic man)

                Manual (21 p.)
                Contents on inside of container lid.
                Summary:  For use in teaching profit and loss, beginning
                budgeting, and supply and demand.



                1. Economics.
```

Care, handling, and storage
See General Guidelines for the Storage of
Three-Dimensional Media on page 93.

Globes

Globe: a sphere with a representation or a map of the earth or the universe. *Relief globes* indicate different heights of land forms by means of a raised surface.

Globes and relief globes are included under this heading and designated by the term Globe.

The rules for Maps on page 49 apply with the following additions and exceptions.

Collation

Number of globes. The word relief is inserted only when the globe has a raised surface. (*See* sample card 60)

Colour.
Diameter of the globe in centimetres or inches.

Notes

Scale is included if known, and is expressed as a representative fraction.

Details about the globe's construction (materials, stand, lighting) may be described if the cataloguer deems this information significant.

Care, handling, and storage

See General Guidelines for the Storage of Three-Dimensional Media on page 93.

Sample card 60

```
912        [World globe]  (Globe)  Replogle  [c1969?]
WOR            1 relief globe.  col.  30 cm. in diameter.  (World nation series)

           1:41,849,600.
           Manual for series (31 p.) by M. Guyette.




           1. Globes.
```

Title supplied by cataloguer.

Note for series manual.

Sample card 61

```
523.43     Mars  (Globe)  Replogle  [1969?]
MAR            1 globe.  col.  15 cm. in diameter.  (World nation series)

           Manual for series (31 p.) by M. Guyette.




           1. Mars.
```

Note for series manual.

Kits

Kit: two or more media, which are not fully interdependent and, therefore, may be used separately.

The medium designation Kit is applied only to those media which are to be catalogued as a unit. A kit may be used effectively as a unit, or its components, which are not fully interdependent, may be used separately.

Two or more interdependent media are not classed as a kit but are catalogued by the dominant medium, with the other media listed in the collation. (*See* sample cards 19-20, 49-53, 108)

A medium of minor or trivial importance, e.g., an ephemeral audiodisc of bird calls attached to the cover of a bird book or a piece of wampum included in a portfolio of Indian documents, may be ignored when selecting the medium designation. Such media may be included in a note or in the collation.

A media centre, which acquires a "kit" composed of two or more media packaged together, may choose to dismantle the set, discard the container, and catalogue each medium under its appropriate designation.

The general rules on pages 13 to 14 apply with the following additions and exceptions.

Main entry
A kit is entered under author where the author has been responsible for the creation of the kit as a whole. If each component has a different author, or if authorship of the kit as a whole cannot be established, enter under title.

Collation
The media are listed alphabetically, together with the number of items in each medium. Physical description of the items is not recommended. If the cataloguer deems the information essential, it may be added.


```
629.2275   Radlauer, Edward.
RAD            Motorcycles  (Kit)  Bowmar, c1967.
                  1 audiodisc, 10 booklets, 1 filmstrip.  (Reading incentive
               program)


               Teacher's guide to series (64 p.)




               1. Motorcycles.  I. Title.  II. Series.
```

Sample card 63

<table>
<tr><td>549
ROC</td><td>Rocks and minerals kit   (Kit)   Dept. of Mines and Technical
Surveys.   Made by National Film Board of Canada [1964?]
1 chart, 3 filmstrips, 1 map, 5 pamphlets, 13 rocks and
minerals.

Manual (53 p.)

1. Mines and mineral resources - Canada.   2. Mineralogy -
Canada.   3. Rocks.</td></tr>
</table>

Sample card 64

<table>
<tr><td>428.81
SOU</td><td>Sounds I can hear   (Kit)   Scott, Foresman, c1966.
4 audiodiscs, 4 charts, 42 flash cards.

Pamphlets attached.
Contents.-   1. House.-   2. Farm in the zoo.-   3. Neighborhood.-
4. School.

1. Reading.   2. Sounds.</td></tr>
</table>

Sample card 65

<table>
<tr><td>N
87
H387</td><td>Hastie, W. Reid.
    Encounter with art   (Kit)   By Reid Hastie and Christian Schmidt.
McGraw-Hill, 1969.
1 book, 100 slides.

1. Art - Psychology.   2. Art - Study and teaching.   I. Schmidt,
Christian.   II. Title.</td></tr>
</table>

```
GN          Anthropology Curriculum Study Project.
27              Patterns in human history  (Kit)  Macmillan, c1971.
A574            2 audiodiscs, 16 blackline masters (in folder) 1 booklet,
            2 filmstrips, 1 transparency (6 overlays)  (Studying societies)

            Teaching plan (44 p.)
            Partial contents.-  Bushmen in the Kalahari desert.-  The Mbuti
        of the Ituri Forest.-  Interview between an anthropologist and a
        Mbuti girl.-  The Malimo and "Tales of the Mbuti".


            1. Anthropology.  I. Title.  II. Series.
```

Partial
contents note.

Care, handling, and storage

See General Guidelines for the Storage of Three-Dimensional Media on page 93.

Machine Readable Data Files

Machine readable data file: information coded by methods that require the use of a machine (typically, but not always, a computer) for translation. Examples include files stored on magnetic tape, punched cards with or without magnetic tape strip, aperture cards, punched paper tapes, disc packs, mark-sensed cards, optical character recognition font documents, etc.

The rules outlined below are based on position papers and minutes prepared by the Subcommittee on Rules for Cataloging Machine Readable Data Files[1] whose findings are still of a tentative nature.

The general rules on pages 13 to 14 apply with the following additions and exceptions.

Main entry

Machine readable data files may contain information of all kinds ranging from poetry to telemetry; however, the majority tend to be of a statistical or tabular nature, often prepared by government or other corporate bodies. In these cases, the rules for citing corporate authors in the *Anglo-American Cataloging Rules* should be consulted.

Title

Machine readable data files usually lack a title page equivalent. The cataloguer may be confronted with no title or many conflicting titles. If conflicting titles are given within the established sources, the title is chosen on the basis of the author's intent, prevalence of use, or citations in reference sources. Dataset names will not usually serve as a title.

Medium designation

The long and cumbersome term "Machine Readable Data File" has been chosen because it is the only term that adequately describes the many formats utilized. The abbreviation "MRDF" may be used if the media centre feels that this abbreviation would be acceptable to its users.

Imprint

The concept of publication does not apply to machine readable data files in the traditional sense. When it is not clear which organization handles the task of processing and releasing the file, it may be necessary to include place and name of several bodies.

Place. Place is recorded when the machine readable data file is not available commercially.

Publisher. The following are considered if the publisher, in the traditional sense, is not discernible:

Producer
Sponsor
Copyright owner
Issuing agent
Funding source
Computer centre responsible
Project group

Date. The date of original release is given. This will frequently have to be approximated. The time period represented by the data, the time period during which the data was collected, and the dates of supplementary files are useful when approximating the original release date, and are given in the notes or summary (see below).

Collation

Since coded information may be transferred easily from one format to another, e.g., punched cards to magnetic tape, the collation should not describe the actual physical format. A statement of the logical records[2] (file size) is given, and amplified as necessary by the notes.[3]

Notes

Source of the title. If the title has been transcribed from any documentation other than the material itself, the source is noted.

Variant titles. Acronymic and catchword titles are noted. Notes for dataset names are optional.

---

[1] American Library Association. Resources and Technical Services Division. Descriptive Cataloging Committee. Subcommittee on Rules for Cataloging Machine Readable Data Files.

[2] *Logical record*: a single unit of information consisting of one or more fields or variables.

[3] A fuller description of a file's physical and technical characteristics as well as of its contents is often recorded in a separate code book or other supplementary documentation, the existence of which is noted on the catalogue card. This is not a recommendation of the Subcommittee on Cataloging Rules for Machine Readable Data Files, but presents an alternate method for handling the present complex collation information.

File size. If the file size has not been verified by machine count, this fact should be
noted.

Restrictions. Restrictions on the use of a
data file are noted.

Summary
The use of a summary outlining content, dates
(see *Date* above) explanation of the collation,
etc., is essential.

Added entries
Added entries are given for acronymic and
catchword titles.

Sample card 67

HN	Davis, James Allen.
29	National data program for the social sciences: Spring, 1972
D385	general social survey (Machine readable data file) Chicago,
	National Opinion Research Center. Distributed by Roper Public
	Opinion Research Center, 1972.
	1613 logical records.

Title from accompanying codebook.
Called also 1972 NORC general social survey.
Size of file not verified.
Summary: Survey of national cross-section of 1613 adults who
answered 61 questions covering such topics as social stratification,

(Continued on next card)

Sample card 67
(continued)

HN	Davis, James Allen.
29	National data program for the social sciences: Spring, 1972
D385	general social survey (Machine readable data file) 1972. (Card 2)

the family, race relations, social control, civil liberties, and morale.

1. Social surveys - United States.   2. United States - Social
conditions.   I. National Opinion Research Center.   II. Title.
III. Title: 1972 NORC general social survey.

JF   Nagel, Stuart.
1043   Redistricting program (Machine readable data file) Ann
N334   Arbor, Mich., Inter-University Consortium for Political Research
            [196-?]
                401 logical records.

                Title from A Guide to resources and services of the Inter-
            University Consortium for Political Research, 1971/72 ed., p. 76.
                Size of file not verified.
                Summary: Input requires descriptions of legal units comprising
            old and new districts together with certain characteristics of each.

                1. Election districts.   2. Electronic data processing -
            Election districts.   I. Title.

Care, handling, and storage

Care, handling, and storage of machine readable data is dependent upon the format of the
file. The data itself can be mechanically transferred from one format to another, e.g.,
punched card to tape. Media centres in the
future will undoubtedly acquire material in one
format and transfer it to any format required.

Some of the formats are discussed on pages
91-93. Specialized publications should be consulted for detailed treatment of this subject.

Maps

Map: a flat representation of part or all of either the earth or the universe. *Relief maps* indicate different heights of land forms by means of a raised surface.

Maps and relief maps are included under this heading and designated by the term Map.

Maps may be organized as ephemeral materials. (*See* pages 97-98) Items of permanent value to the collection should be completely catalogued for their effective use.

This section discusses the cataloguing of maps for an integrated collection. Chapter 11 of the *Anglo-American Cataloging Rules* provides alternate rules of main entry for maps. Appendix A (pages 97-98) gives rules for a specialized collection of maps which are not integrated with other media in the catalogue or on the shelves.

The general rules on pages 13 to 14 apply with the following additions and exceptions.

Main entry
Maps are entered under title. Some maps may be entered under cartographer if a media centre deems it important to link bibliographically the cartographer's books, maps, and other works.

If two or more titles are given on the face of the map, preference is given in the following order:
1) the most appropriate title;
2) the title within the border of the map;
3) the title in the margin.

If no title appears on the face of the map, a title is supplied in square brackets from accompanying material or outside sources.

For more explicit instructions on establishing map titles, see Rule 212A, *Anglo-American Cataloging Rules*.

Author statement
Cartographer, surveyor, or engraver is noted if this information is considered to be important.

Collation
Number of sheets. If the sheets are printed on both sides, this information is noted in parenthesis. When relief is indicated by a raised surface, the term relief map replaces sheet. (*See* sample card 74)
Colour.
Size of the inside border in centimetres or inches.

Notes
Scale. Where possible, scale should be expressed as a representative fraction, e.g., 1:1,000,000. (Natural scale indicators for conversion of graphic scales to representative fractions are commercially available.)
Prime meridian, if other than Greenwich, is noted.
Projection. Note on type of projection is optional.


```
936.204    Ordnance survey map of Roman Britain   (Map)   3d ed.
ORD            Chessington, Surrey, Director-General of the Ordnance
               Survey, 1956.
               1 sheet.  col.  97 x 75 cm.

               1:1,000,000.
               Conical projection.
               Inset map of Shetland and Orkney Islands.
               All known Roman sites shown.

               1. Gt. Brit. - History - Roman period, 55 B.C. - 449 A.D.
```

917
VAC

Vacationlands of the United States and Southern Canada   (Map)
National Geographic Society, 1966.
1 sheet (printed both sides)   col.   25 x 37 in.

1: 5,132,160.
Albers conical equal-area projection.
9 insets.
Index to parks.

1. National parks and reserves - U.S.   2. National parks and
reserves - Canada.   I. National Geographic Society, Washington, D.C.

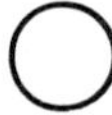

Sample card 70

914.5632
PIA

Pianta di Roma   (Map)   Touring Club Italiano, 1962.
1 sheet.   col.   86 x 78 cm.

Index (16 p.)
1: 12,000.
Summary: Shows streets, major buildings, rivers, parks, built-up
areas of Rome.

1. Rome (City) - Description.

Sample card 71

Title in Italian.

915.9
SOU

South-east Asia   (Map)   Bartholomew, 1966.
1 sheet.   col.   68 x 88 cm.

1: 5,800,000.
Mercator projection.
Inset map of Malaya, 1:3,000,000.

1. Asia, Southeastern - Description and travel.   2. Malaya -
Description and travel.

Sample card 72

Scale of inset
map.

915.67   Tourist map of Iraq (Map) [Baghdad] Summer Resorts and
TOU   Tourism Service [196-?]
              1 sheet (printed both sides) col. 63 x 60 cm.

              1: 1,550,000.
              Summary: Shows roads, railroads, pipelines, relief,
       archaelogical centres, administrative centres.

              1. Iraq - Description and travel.

912   Plastic relief map of the world (Map) Educational Aids
PLA   Publishing Corp., c1963.
              1 relief map. col. 47 x 67 cm.

              1:1,013,760.
              Mercator projection.

              1. World maps.

Topographic series of maps

A topographic series is a group of sheets, depicting general physical and cultural details, in which contiguous areas are mapped in the same scale and in accordance with a uniform set of symbols and mapping standards. The relation of one sheet to another is usually indicated by a small scale index map.

Topographic sheets in a series are not listed individually in the catalogue. Only the top or index sheet is listed. The index sheet is consulted to find the individual sheets in the series.

The index sheet may be fully catalogued. An easier and adequate method of catalogue listing is by reference entry, as shown below.

Sample card 75

Canada.   Topographic series.   1:250,000.

To find maps held in this series, see map drawer 6,
index sheet no. 18

The individual maps in the series held by the media centre and their respective locations are indicated on the index sheet.

Care, handling, and storage
See General Guidelines for the Care, Handling, and Storage of Two-Dimensional, Opaque Materials on page 93.

Microforms

Microform: a miniature reproduction of printed or other graphic matter which cannot be utilized without magnification.

Microfilm, microfiche, micro-opaques, and aperture cards are included under this heading and designated by the term Microform.

The *Anglo-American Cataloging Rules* treats the microform as a book, describing the original document in the body of the card and the microform in a note. This approach does not require the use of a medium designation. Many media centres with multi-media catalogues will wish to catalogue microforms in conformance with other nonbook materials, i.e., describe the microform format in the body of the card and the original format in a note. If this policy is adopted, the following rules should be used.

The general rules on pages 13 to 14 apply with the following additions and exceptions.

Collation

Physical description is in the following order:

APERTURE CARDS
Number of aperture cards.
Size of the mount in centimetres.

FILM
Number of film reels, cartridges or cassettes.
Size. Width of the film in millimetres.

FICHE
Number of fiche.
Size of sheet in centimetres.

OPAQUE CARDS
Number of opaque cards.
Size of card in centimetres.

Notes
Notes are listed in the following order:
1. *Reduction ratio.* Most microform readers in common use in media centres can accommodate materials with a 16-30 x reduction. A reduction ratio outside this range should be noted using the following terms extracted from the *Glossary of Micrographics* published by the National Microfilm Association:
Low reduction – up to and inclusive of 15 x.
High reduction – 31 x to 60 x.
Very high reduction – 61 x to 90 x. (*See* sample card 79)
Ultra high reduction – above 90 x. In this range the specific ratio is also given. (*See* sample card 80)
2. *Container.* The name of the producer of cassette or cartridge containers is noted, because containers are not interchangeable in every reader. (*See* sample card 81)
3. *Original format.* If the microform was published originally in another format, the bibliographic details of this publication are noted. (*See* sample cards 76-81)
4. *Positive reproductions* are not noted.

Sample card 76

```
Z            Wilkinson, John Provost.
736              A history of Dalhousie University Main Library, 1867-1931
H34              (Microform)  Dept. of Photoduplication, University of Chicago
W545         Library, 1966.
                 1 film reel.  35 mm.

                 Thesis - University of Chicago, 1966.  280 l.  illus.
                 Bibliography: l. 276-280.


             1. Dalhousie University.  Library - History.
```

Microfilm.
Original format.

Sample card 77

<pre>
Z   Atherton, Pauline.
695.9   Aid-to-indexing forms; a progress report ...   (Microform)
A844   American Institute of Physics, Documentation Research Project.
           1963.
               1 fiche.   10 x 15 cm.   (AIP/DRP 63-2)

               Collation of original: 14, 4 l.

               1. Indexing.   I. American Institute of Physics.   Documentation
           Research Project.   II. Title.
</pre>

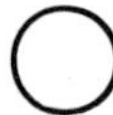

Microfiche.

Sample card 78

<pre>
E   Kellogg, Louise Phelps.
131   Early narratives of the Northwest   (Microform)   Microcard
K445   Corp., 1963.
               5 opaque cards.   8 x 13 cm.

               Originally published by T.J. Brown, 1865.   106 p.

               1. America - Discovery and exploration - French.   2. Northwest,
           Old - Discovery and exploration.   I. Title.
</pre>

Micro-opaque.

Sample card 79

<pre>
BF   James, William, 1842-1920.
121   The principles of psychology   (Microform)   Library
J2   Resources, c1970.
1891a   2 fiche.   8 x 13 cm.

               Very high reduction.
               Originally published by Macmillan, 1891.   2 v.

               1. Psychology.
</pre>

Microfiche.
Cutter number.
Reduction ratio.

Sample card 80

E   Craven, John Joseph.
467.1   Prison life of Jefferson Davis (Microform) National Cash
D26   Register [196-?]
C9   1 fiche. 10 x 15 cm. (PMCI collection)
1866a

          Ultra high reduction, 150 x.
          Originally published by Carleton, c1866. 377 p.
          With Force, M. General Sherman. McClennan, H. Life and
campaigns of Major-General J.E.B. Stuart. Parton, J. General
Butler in New Orleans. Poore, B. Life and public services of
Ambrose E. Burnside. Bache, R. Life of Gen. George G. Meade.

      1. Davis, Jefferson.   I. Title.

Microfiche.

Reduction ratio.

"With" note.

Sample card 81

Z   Special libraries (Microform) *v. 59-61, 1968-70*
671   University Microfilms.
S71   *1* film cartridges. 35 mm.

         For Information Design reader.
         Official journal of the Special Libraries Association.
         Originally published by the Special Libraries Association
New York.

      1. Libraries, Special - Periodicals. I. Special Libraries
Association.

Microfilm in
cartridge.

Open entry.

Care, handling, and storage
See General Guidelines for the Care, Handling,
and Storage of Film Media on page 92.

Microscope Slides

Microscope slide: a specialized slide produced specifically for use with a microscope.

Microscope slides may be organized in slide trays (see pages 81-82). Items of permanent value to the collection should be completely catalogued for their effective use.

The general rules on pages 13 to 14 apply with the following additions and exceptions.

Imprint
Because most microscope slides contain realia, the date is not necessary in the imprint.

Collation
Number of slides.

Type of mount in parenthesis.
Colour is noted only if the slide is stained. (See sample cards 82, 84)
Size of the mount in centimetres.

Notes
The following notes may be required for extensive microscope slide collections at advanced academic levels:

Colour and type of stain.

The particular aspect of the slide the stain highlights. (See sample card 84)

If the slide is intended for use with other than a phase or interference microscope, the type of microscope to be used is noted.

Sample card 82

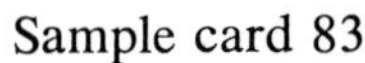

Sample card 83

```
632.4      Apple scab   (Microscope slide)   A. Reid Enterprises.
APP        18 slides (glass)   3 x 8 cm.

           Classroom set containing similar sections of the scab.




           1. Apple scab.
```

Sample card 84

```
591.47     Cartilage in rabbit ear   (Microscope slide)   Ward's Natural
CAR        Science Establishment.
           1 slide (glass)   stained.   3 x 8 cm.

           Stained black with Weigert's stain to show elastic fibres.




           1. Cartilage.
```

Care, handling, and storage

See General Guidelines for the Care, Handling,
and Storage of Microscope Slides on page 92.

Models

Model: a three-dimensional representation of an object, either exact or to scale; a mock-up.

The general rules on pages 13 to 14 apply with the following additions and exceptions.

Collation

Number of pieces (the use of the term "various pieces" is optional).

Colour (one or two specific colours may be listed, if applicable).

Size. Dimensions in centimetres or inches are included where applicable.

Notes

Notes are often essential to indicate use.

Sample card 85

```
611.71     Human skeleton model  (Model)  Ideal School Supply Co.,
HUM        1964.
           2 pieces.  white.  30 cm.  (Human anatomy group, S228)

           Notes by Jack Megenity.
           Plastic scale model with stand.




           1. Bones.  2. Skeleton.  I. Series.
```

Sample card 86

```
574.8732   The Molecule of life  (Model)  Silver Burdett, c1964.
MOL        various pieces.  col.

           Manual entitled: DNA: the molecule of life, by S. Pestka and
           T. Woudenberg.
           Title on outer container: DNA-RNA protein synthesis model kit.
           Pieces can be arranged to produce the DNA helix, DNA replication,
           and DNA and RNA polypeptide synthesis.

           1. Deoxyribonucleic acid.  2. Ribonucleic acid.  I. Title: DNA:
           the molecule of life.  II. Title: DNA-RNA protein synthesis model kit.
```

Alternate titles noted.

Added entries made for alternate titles.

493.1   Rosetta stone unit   (Model)   Consultant: Edward L.B. Terrace.
ROS   Alva Museum Replicas, 1965.
             1 piece. black. 30 x 23 x 5 cm.

             Class set of Student's activity sheet.
             Teacher's manual (8 p.)

             1. Rosetta stone inscription.   I. Terrace, Edward L.B.

Care, handling, and storage
See General Guidelines for the Storage of
Three-Dimensional Media on page 93.

Motion Pictures

Motion picture: film, with or without sound track, bearing a sequence of images which create the illusion of movement when projected.

Loops, cartridges, cassettes, kinescopes, etc., are included under this heading and designated by the term Motion picture.

The general rules on pages 13 to 14 apply with the additions and exceptions noted below. Media centres requiring more detailed cataloguing of motion pictures are referred to the *Anglo-American Cataloging Rules*, Chapter 12.

Main entry

Motion pictures are entered under title. The difficulty of ascribing authorship in motion picture production mitigates against author entry. Exceptions to this rule may be made in adherence to the "auteur" theory, or where it is desirable that the book and the motion picture be cited together in the catalogue (e.g., Sir Kenneth Clark's *Civilisation*).

Title

Title and subtitle are transcribed as they appear on the title frames.

Imprint

Sponsor[1], if any, is given in distinctive abridged form directly after the medium designation.
Producer[1] is given next, also in distinctive abridged form. If a sponsor is involved, the producer information is preceded by the phrase "Made by."
Releasing agent, if different from the producer, is given next in distinctive abridged form, preceded by the phrase "Released by."
Date. Date of release follows the name of the releasing agent. If the date of production differs significantly from the date of release, the production date follows the name of the producer. These dates are often difficult to interpret from the film itself. Secondary sources such as pro-

---

[1] The *Anglo-American Cataloging Rules* gives the following definitions:
Sponsor: The company, institution, organization, or individual who brings a motion picture into existence, not directly, but by the employment of a production company.
Producer: The company, institution, organization or individual who exercises the immediate overall responsibility for the physical processes involved in making a motion picture.

ducers' catalogues will be useful in providing this essential information.

Collation

Physical description is given in the following order:
Number of cartridges or cassettes, if applicable.
Duration in minutes.
Sound or silent.
Colour.
Size. Width of the film is given in millimetres. Super 8 film must be so described.
Series statement. Terms such as "episode," "part," etc., are indicated by the abbreviation "no."

Notes

Notes are given in the following order:
Supplementary collation information. Special equipment required for projection (e.g., three-dimensional film, magnetic sound track) and/or unusual physical features (e.g., kinescope recording, Technicolor, etc.) should be indicated.
Production credits are given at the cataloguer's discretion, and listed in the following order:
  Producer(s) if not already given in the imprint.
  Director(s)
  Film editor(s)
  Collaboration authorities
  Cinematographer or director of photography
  Writer(s)
  Narrator(s)
  Individual(s) responsible for music
Other individuals are included only if their contribution is of special significance.
Cast credits are given at the cataloguer's discretion and listed in order of billing. More than five are noted only if especially significant.

Summary

An objective and succinct summary of the content and intended use of the film is essential. Audience level may be included either within the body of the summary or added as a separate sentence at the end. (See page 14 for the list of terms for audience level)

Added entries

Sponsors, producers and releasing agents should be traced.

915.1132   China: cities in transition   (Motion picture)   Doubleday Multi-
CHI   media, 1969.
         1 cartridge.   18 min.   sd.   col.   Super 8 mm.   (Red China series)

        Technicolor cartridge.
        Notes on cartridge case.
        Summary: The growth and nature of Shanghai are shown with
contrasts between traditional and modern modes of life.

        1. Shanghai - Description.   2. Housing - China (People's
Republic of China, 1949-   )   I. Doubleday Multimedia.

Cartridge film.

531.112   Finding the speed of a rifle bullet   (Motion picture)   National
FIN   Film Board of Canada,   1968.
         1 cartridge.   3 min.   si.   col.   Super 8 mm.   (Project physics)

        Kodak cartridge.
        Notes on cartridge case.
        Summary: Shows the procedure utilized in calculating bullet
speed.

        1. Kinematics.   I. National Film Board of Canada.

Super 8 mm.

909.826   The World of '68   (Motion picture)   Charles Braverman.
WOR   Released by Pyramid Film Producers, c1969.
         5 min.   sd.   col.   Super 8 mm.

        Magnetic sound.
        Credits: Camera, Sylvia Dees; Production assistant, Ken
Rudolph.
        Summary: A kinestasis film using kaleidoscopic views of still
pictures to summarize the year 1968.

        1. Newsreels - 1968.   I. Braverman, Charles.   II. Pyramid Film
Producers.

The same film
released in
different formats.

Super 8 mm.

Special equipment
necessary.

Sample card 90B

909.826 The World of '68 (Motion picture) Charles Braverman.
WOR   Released by Pyramid Film Producers, c1969.
                 5 min. sd. col. 16 mm.

        Credits: Camera, Sylvia Dees; Production assistant, Ken
Rudolph.
        Summary: A kinestasis film using kaleidoscopic views of still
p i ctures to summarize the year 1968.

        1. Newsreels - 1968.   I. Braverman, Charles.   II. Pyramid Film
Producers.

16 mm. format.

Sample card 91

551.375 Dunes (Motion picture) David Adams. Released by Pyramid
DUN   Film Producers, 1968.
                 7 min. sd. col. 16 mm.

        Credits: Filmed & edited by Fred Hudson; Music, Michel
Michelet.
        Summary: Shows the changing world of the sand dunes and
th e ir inhabitants.

        1. Sand-dunes. I. Hudson, Fred.   II. Adams, David.
III. Pyramid Film Producers.

Sample card 92

155.532 Skaterdater (Motion picture) Marshal Backlar, 1965.
SKA   Released by Pyramid Films, 1971.
                 18 min. sd. col. 16 mm.

        Credits: Director, editor, writer, Noel Black; Photographer,
M i chael Murphy; Music, Nick Venet and Mike Curb.
        Summary: Portrays a boy's emergence into adolescence as he
s l ow ly realizes that his skateboard gang is part of a childhood
t h a t he has outgrown.

        1. Adolescence. I. Backlar, Marshal.   II. Black, Noel.
I I I. Pyramid Film Producers.

Sample card 93

<table>
<tr><td>614.88
ART</td><td>Artificial respiration (Motion picture) Moreland-Latchford
Productions, 1965.
8 min. sd. col. 16 mm. (Survival in the wilderness, no. 5)</td></tr>
</table>

Summary: Close-up illustration of mouth-to-mouth resuscitation and the recently approved manual technique - the Sylvester method.

1. Artificial respiration. I. Moreland-Latchford Productions. II. Series.

Sample card 94

<table>
<tr><td>791.4309
FUN</td><td>The Fun factory (Motion picture) Paul Killiam and Saul J.
Turrell. Released by Gregstone Enterprises, c1959.
30 min. sd. b&w. 16 mm. (The History of the motion picture series)</td></tr>
</table>

Summary: Mack Sennett's development of slap-stick as a comedy form, and his creation of such stars as Ben Turpin, Carole Lombard, Charlie Chaplin, and Marie Dressler.

1. Moving-pictures - History. 2. Sennett, Mack. I. Killiam, Paul. II. Turrell, Saul J. III. Gregstone Enterprises. IV. Series.

Sample card 95

<table>
<tr><td>977
RIS</td><td>The Rise and fall of the Great Lakes (Motion picture)
National Film Board of Canada, 1969.
17 min. sd. col. 16 mm.</td></tr>
</table>

Credits: Producer, Joseph Koenig; director, script writer and photographer, William Mason; scientific adviser, V.K. Prest; music director, Robert Fleming; animation cameraman, Kjeld Nielsen.

Summary: A lone canoeist lives through all the changes of geological history, through Ice Age and flood, only to find himself trapped in the end in a sea of scum.

1. Great Lakes. I. Mason, William. II. National Film Board of Canada.

Sample card 96

791.43 The Rink (Motion Picture) Mutual Film Corp., 1916. Released
RIN   by Blackhawk Films/Eastin-Phelan Corp. [196-?]
          22 min. si. b&w. 16 mm.

          Credits: Producer and writer, Charles Chaplin. Cast: Charlie
          Chaplin, Edna Purviance, James T. Kelly, Eric Campbell, and others.
          Summary: A slapstick comedy about Charlie, a waiter, and his
          experiences at the roller-skating rink where he spends most of his
          time.

          I. Chaplin, Charles. II. Eastin-Phelan Corporation. III. Mutual
          Film Corporation.

Sample card 97

291.178 From the ashes (Motion picture) Canadian Broadcasting Corp.,
FRO   1970.
          26 min. sd. b&w. 16 mm. (Man alive)

          Kinescope recording.
          Summary: Jewish author Elie Wiesel discusses his views on
          God, Christianity, Judaism, the plight of man in society and the
          Jewish experience in Nazi extermination camps.

          1. Wiesel, Eliezer. 2. Church and social problems. 3. Judaism and
          social problems. 4. God. I. Canadian Broadcasting Corporation.
          II. Series.

Kinescope
recording.

Care, handling, and storage
See General Guidelines for the Care, Handling,
and Storage of Film Media on page 92.

Pictures

Picture: a two-dimensional drawing, painting, portrait, photograph, or a print of any of these, produced on an opaque backing.

Pictures, art originals, art prints, photographs, post cards, posters, and study prints are included under this heading and designated by the term Picture.

Pictures may be organized in a picture file (*see* pages 81-82). Items of permanent value to the collection should be completely catalogued for their effective use.

The general rules on pages 13 to 14 apply with the following additions and exceptions.

Collation
Number and type of picture.
Colour.
Size in centimetres or inches. Size of the actual print is given for art originals and prints, size of the mount for all other pictures.

Notes
Methods of reproduction and mounting may be noted for art prints.


```
301.34    Owen, Edward E.
OWE           Families and communities  (Picture)  Fitzhenry & Whiteside,
          c1972.
              96 photos.  col.  54 x 42 cm.  (Discussion picture programme
          f o r elementary school studies, year 2)

              Teacher's manual (155 p.)
              Contents.-  a. Communities are social units which may differ.-
          b. The community serves many functions.-  c. The community is
          a network of relationships.-  d. Communities change.

              1. Community life.  I. Title.
```

Photograph.


```
971.2     Historical Services and Consultants.
HIS           A picture study of the settlement of the West  (Picture)
          Prepared by Historical Services and Consultants under the
          d i rection of John T. Saywell and John C. Ricker.  Burns &
          MacEachern [196-?]
              25 study prints.  b&w.  28 x 35 cm.

              1. The West, Canadian - Descr. & trav.  I. Saywell, John T.
          II. Ricker, John C.  III. Title.
```

Study print.

Sample card 100

<pre>
599   Weber, Walter Alois.
WEB   Wild animals (Picture) Donohue [1934]
              12 pictures. col. 12 x 10 in.

              Illustrations from the book entitled Homes and habits of
           wild animals, by K.P. Schmidt, Donohue, c1934.
              Contents.- Caribou.- Beavers.- Wolverine.- Badger.- Opossum.-
           Bats, kangaroo rats, armadillo.- Snowshoe rabbit.- Marten.- Jaguar.-
           Fox.- Otter.- Giant bear.

              1. Animals. I. Schmidt, Karl Patterson. Homes and habits of
           wild animals. II. Title.
</pre>

Picture.

Sample card 101

<pre>
913.377   Historical reconstructions of Pompeii (Picture)
H629   Encyclopaedia Britannica, c1965.
              4 study prints. col. 33 x 45 cm. (History series)

              Each print has attached overlay.
              Text on verso.
              Teacher's study guide card.
              Contents.- The House of the Faun.- The pistrinum (bakery)-
           The theater.- The Temple of Apollo.

              1. Pompeii - Antiquities, Roman. 2. Architecture, Roman.
</pre>

Study print.

Cutter number.

Sample card 102

<pre>
759.4   Degas, Hilaire Germain Edgar.
DEG   Two dancers on the stage (Picture) Shorewood Publishers,
           c1960.
              1 art print. col. 60 x 48 cm.

              Unmounted lithograph.

              1. Ballet. 2. Impressionism (Art) 3. Paintings, French.
           I . Title.
</pre>

Art print.

Care, handling, and storage
See General Guidelines for the Care, Handling, and Storage of Two-Dimensional, Opaque Materials on page 93.

Realia

Realia: actual objects; artifacts, samples, specimens.

The general rules on pages 13 to 14 apply with the following additions and exceptions.

Imprint
Date is not given, unless this information is significant. (*See* sample card 104)

Collation
Number of pieces.
Other information discussed under Collation in the General Rules (pages 13-14) is listed only if necessary to the proper identification of an item.

Notes
If the physical description cannot be given concisely in the collation, the collation statement is amplified in the notes.

Care, handling, and storage
See General Guidelines for the Storage of Three-Dimensional Media on page 93.

Sample card 103

```
549.66      Asbestos  (Realia)  Johns-Manville.
ASB            4 pieces.




            1. Asbestos.
```

Sample card 104

```
391         [Mohawk Indian costume]  (Realia)  [186-?]
MOH            5 pieces.

            Includes headdress, beaded shirt, trousers, and moccasins.




            1. Mohawk Indians.
```

Slides

Slide: a small unit of transparent material containing an image, mounted in rigid format and designed for use in a slide viewer or projector. Presentation of special slides in pairs (stereographs) produces a three-dimensional effect.

Slides and stereographs are included under this heading and designated by the term Slide.

Slides may be organized in slide trays (*see* pages 81-82). Items of permanent value to the collection should be completely catalogued for their effective use.

The general rules on pages 13 to 14 apply with the following additions and exceptions.

Collation
Physical description is given in the following order:

SLIDES
Number of slides. If the slide is made of glass, the word glass in parenthesis follows the number of slides, e.g., 1 slide (glass).
Colour.
Size of the mount in centimetres or inches.

STEREOGRAPHS
Number of stereographs or stereograph cards.
Number of double frames, given in parenthesis, is optional.
Colour.
Size of the mount in centimetres or inches should be given if this is not implicit in the name of the producer.

551.31   Glacial landforms (Slide) National Film Board of Canada and
G45   Dept. of Energy, Mines and Resources, c1970.
              46 slides. col. 2 x 2 in.

              Manual (50 p.) by Jack Ives.

       1. Landforms. 2. Glaciology. I. Canada. Dept. of Energy, Mines and Resources.

Sample card 105

Slide set.

Cutter number.

759.9492   Rembrandt Hermanszoon van Rijn.
REM   A girl with a broom   (Slide)   Washington, D.C.,
           National Gallery of Art [195-?]
               1 slide. col. 2 x 2 in.

           Andrew Mellon Collection.

           1. Paintings, Dutch.   I. Title.

387.734   Airplanes of the world   (Slide)   View-Master [196-?]
AIR   3 stereograph cards. col.

           "Story booklet" (16 p.)

           1. Aeroplanes.

531.1   Matter and energy   (Slide)   View-Master, c1969.
MAT   3 stereograph cards (7 double fr. each) col. (Physics)
           (View-Master science series)

           "Story booklet" (16 p.)

           1. Force and energy.

Sample card 109

709.034   Evans, Grose.
EVA   19th century developments in art (Slide) Society for Visual
           Education, c1969.
            40 slides. col. 2 x 2 in., and 1 audiodisc (30 min.)

           1. Art - Hist. - 19th century. I. Title.

Slide with
interdependent
accompanying
medium.

Care, handling, and storage

See General Guidelines for the Care, Handling,
and Storage of Film Media on page 92.

Transparencies

Transparency: an image produced on transparent material, designed for use with an overhead projector.

Transparencies may be organized as ephemeral materials (*see* pages 81-82). Items of permanent value to the collection should be completely catalogued for their effective use.

The general rules on pages 13 to 14 apply with the following additions and exceptions.

Collation
Number of sheets, followed by the number of attached overlays in parenthesis, if applicable. *Colour.*
Size of the transparency in centimetres or inches, excluding mount.

Notes
Notes are sometimes essential to indicate use.

<table>
<tr><td>

```
529        Clock  (Transparency)  Visucom Projectuals, c1960.
CLO        1 sheet (5 attached overlays)  col.  10 x 12 in.

           Dial transparency used to teach how to tell time.




           1. Clocks and watches.
                              ◯
```

</td><td>

Sample card 110

Abridged Dewey decimal classification.

Sears subject headings.

</td></tr>
</table>

<table>
<tr><td>

```
516.13     From sets of points to geometric constructions  (Transparency)
FRO        Colonial Films, c1967.
           12 sheets (attached overlays)  col.  19 x 25 cm.




           1. Geometry.
                          ◯
```

</td><td>

Sample card 111

</td></tr>
</table>

Sample card 112

```
325.344097
FRE        French colonies in America.  Colonies françaises d'Amérique
           (Transparency)  National Film Board of Canada, c1968.
           1 sheet  (3 attached overlays)  col.  19 x 25 cm.

           English/French text by Roland Lamontagne.




           1. France - Colonies - North America.
```

Sample card 113

```
551.6971   Climate and weather.  Climats  (Transparency)  NFBC, c1969.
CLI        4 sheets.  col.  19 x 25 cm.  (Geographical maps of Canada)




           1. Canada - Climate.  I. Series.
```

Producer in
abbreviated
form.

Care, handling, and storage

See General Guidelines for the Care, Handling, and Storage of Film Media on page 92. Additional storage suggestions for transparencies will be found under General Guidelines for the Care, Handling, and Storage of Two-Dimensional Opaque Materials on page 93.

Videorecords

Videorecord: a recording designed for television playback.

Tapes, discs, and electronic video recordings are included under this heading and designated by the term Videorecord.

Many videotapes are taped by libraries and educational systems for temporary use and will be erased at some future date. These tapes can be treated as ephemeral materials and need not be catalogued. Items of permanent value to the collection should be completely catalogued for their effective use.

The rules for Motion Pictures on pages 60 to 64 apply to videorecords with the following additions and exceptions.

Title

Videorecords of original material with distinctive titles are entered under these titles. However, many videotapes are recordings of broadcast television programs, which list only the series title, e.g., *Man at the centre*. In these cases, a title for each program must be supplied by the cataloguer. (*See* sample card 114)

The title on some videorecords is presented orally rather than visually. This title is used in the absence of a written title.

The *Anglo-American Cataloging Rules* should be consulted for rules governing title changes and alternate titles.

Imprint

The date on the videorecord is listed immediately after the name of the producer. If no date appears on the videorecord, the first broadcast date, if known, may be used.

Collation

Physical description is given in the following order:

TAPE
Number or portion of tapes, tape cassettes, or tape cartridges.
Duration.
Sound or silent. This information is given only in the rare instance where the sound track has not been used. The notation "si." is used in such cases.
Colour.
Size. The width of the tape is given in inches. At the present time (1972) the width of the tape is implicit in the name and model number of the recording equipment, and, therefore not

required. However, standardization of video recording systems is anticipated. (The Electronics Industries Association of Japan have set a standard for ½ inch videotape recorders.) As standardization is achieved, the information necessary will include the tape width and not the recording machinery.
Playback speed. If the video recording machine by which a tape has been made can record at different speeds, the playback speed is given. If the video recording machine tapes only at one speed, this information is implicit in the name of the video recorder and, therefore, not necessary.
Recording mode. Helical videotape systems are not noted. The quadruplex system, used by television broadcast stations, is not generally acquired by media centres in the original quadruplex videotape format. If a quadruplex videotape is catalogued, the collation will list: number of tapes, time, colour, size, speed, recording mode, i.e., quadruplex.

DISCS[1]
Number of discs.
Duration.
Colour.
Size of disc in inches.
Playback speed. At the present time (1972) playback speed need not be given, since only one company is producing videodiscs, which are of uniform speed. However, if in the future other firms produce videodiscs with different playback speeds, this information will become an essential element in the collation. Media centres which anticipate a large collection of videodiscs should add playback speed.

ELECTRONIC VIDEO RECORDINGS and OTHER FILM FORMATS
Number of film cassettes or cartridges.
Duration.
Sound or silent.
Colour.
Size. Width of the film is given in millimetres.

Notes

A media centre which must list detailed technical information in its catalogue should request data sheets from producers.

---

[1] Rules for videodiscs, which have not yet been marketed in North America, are tentative.

Supplementary collation information is given in the following order:

TAPES
Special equipment required for playback. The make and model number of the video recording machine is given. (*See* sample cards 115-120. This information is unnecessary for quadruplex videotapes.) For quadruplex or Ampex 1-inch tapes, high or low band must be noted. (*See* sample card 114)
Field and Colour Standards. If a media centre intends to participate in any international bibliographic control of videotapes, the cataloguing information should note line and field standards and colour standards. In North America the line and field standards are generally 525 lines and 60 fields (expressed as 525/60). In Britain, Europe, Australia, and New Zealand this standard is 625/50. In North America the colour standard is NTSC; in Britain, Australia, New Zealand and Germany it is PAL; in France and Russia it is SECAM, etc. (*See* sample cards 116, 117)

DISCS
Line, field, and colour standards are listed as above, if applicable.

ELECTRONIC VIDEO RECORDINGS and OTHER FILM FORMATS
Special equipment required for playback. A trade name may be given, e.g., CBS Electronic Video Recording. (*See* sample card 122)

Sample card 114

```
921.2      [Bertrand Russell interview]  (Videorecord)  Canadian
R911           Broadcasting Corp., 1970.
               1 tape.  30 min.  b&w.  1 in.  (Man at the centre)


           Ampex 7500C.  High band.
           Summary: A 1959 interview with 86 year old Lord Russell
        i n which his biographical reminiscences and the rationality of those
        who head power blocks are discussed.



           1. Russell, Bertrand Russell, 3d Earl.  I. Series.
```

Tape.

Cutter number.

Sample card 115

```
812        W i l d e r, Thornton Niven.
WIL            Infancy.  Childhood  (Videorecord)  National Educational
           T elevision, 1970.
               1 tape.  90 min.  b&w.  1 in.  (A Generation of leaves)
           (P layhouse)


           Shibaden SV-727.
           Credits:  Cast, Fred Gwynne, Eileen Brennan.
           Summary:  Two one-act serio-comic plays about the failure
        o f generations to communicate.

           I. Title.  II. Title: Childhood.  III. Series.  IV. Series: Playhouse.
```

Tape.

Sample card 116

```
340.11    The Administration of justice  (Videorecord)  Ontario
ADM           Educational Communications Authority, 1970.
              1 tape.  18 min.  col.  1 in.  (Law)

              Sony EV-320.  525/60; NTSC.
              Credits:  Producer, Wally Longul; writer, William Davidson.
              Summary:  Interviews with the Federal Minister of Justice,
          the Attorney General of Ontario, and two Chief Justices.




              1. Justice, Administration of.
```

Tape.

Line, field, and colour standard noted.

Sample card 117

```
153.83    Decision making  (Videorecord)  Ontario Educational
DEC           Communications Authority, 1970.
              1 tape.  30 min.  b&w.  1/2 in.  (Insights of psychology)

              Panasonic NV 8100.
              Summary:  Examines the process involved in rational decision-
          making and  emotional reaction.




              1. Reasoning (Psychology)  2. Choice (Psychology)  3. Psychology.
          I . Series.
```

Tape.

Sample card 118

```
621.381534
PUL       Pulse generator basics  (Videorecord)  Hewlett-Packard, 1970.
              1 tape cassette.  24 min.  b&w.  3/4 in.

              Sony Videocassette.  525/60.
              Summary:  Illustrates a device which produces a signal that
          switches between 2 DC levels.




              1. Oscillators, Electric.
```

Tape cassette.

Line and field standard noted.

<table>
<tr><td>

770.28
PHO

The Photographic model (Videorecord) CTV, 1970.
    1/2 tape. 30 min. b&w. 1 in. (Photography, part 3)
(University of the air)

    Panasonic NV504.
    With: Color photography (Videorecord)
    Summary: Illustrates the correct way to arrange a photographic
set; model posture; grooming; posing, etc.

       1. Models, Artists'. 2. Photography - Techniques. I. Series.
II. Series: University of the air.

</td><td>

Sample card 119

Portion of tape.

Producer in abbreviated form.

"With" note.

</td></tr>
</table>

<table>
<tr><td>

770.28
PHO

Color photography (Videorecord) CTV, 1970.
    1/2 tape. 30 min. b&w. 1 in. (Photography, part 5)
(University of the air)

    Panasonic NV504.
    With: The Photographic model (Videorecord)
    Summary: Reviews primary and secondary colours, and those
compositional factors relating primarily to colour photography.

       1. Color photography. I. Series. II. Series: University of the air.

</td><td>

Sample card 120

Portion of tape.

Producer in abbreviated form.

"With" note.

</td></tr>
</table>

<table>
<tr><td>

599.0994
MAM

Mammals of Australia (Videorecord) Teldec, 1972.
    1 disc. 5 min. b&w. 9 in. 1500 rpm.

    625/50.
    Narrated by John Smith.

       1. Mammals - Australia.

</td><td>

Sample card 121

Disc.

</td></tr>
</table>

Sample card 122

977   The Rise and fall of the Great Lakes (Videorecord) National
RIS   Film Board of Canada, 1969.
              1 film cassette. 17 min. sd. col. 9 mm.

              CBS Electronic Video Recording.
              Credits: Producer, Joseph Koenig; director, script writer, and
photographer, William Mason; scientific advisor, V.K. Prest;
music director, Robert Flemming; animation cameraman, Kjeld
Nielsen.
              Summary: A lone canoeist lives through all the changes of
geological history, through Ice Age and flood, only to find himself
trapped in the end in a sea of scum.
         1. Great Lakes.   I. Mason, William. II. National Film
Board of Canada.

Film.

Care, handling, and storage
Tape. See General Guidelines for the Care, Handling, and Storage of Magnetic Tape on page 92.
Discs. The manufacturer's advertisements emphasize the durability of videodiscs. They appear to require no special care for normal media centre handling and storage. After videodiscs have been marketed commercially, guidelines for their care, handling, and storage will be investigated.
Film. See General Guidelines for the Care, Handling, and Storage of Film Media on page 92.

References to Materials Not Listed in the Catalogue   3

Ephemeral Materials, Vertical Files, and Picture Files

Not all media centre materials warrant the expenditure involved in complete cataloguing and processing. The media specialist must decide whether the format of the material is durable enough to withstand normal use and whether the content of the material is valuable enough to add to the centre's permanent collection. Newspaper clippings, pamphlets, single un-mounted pictures and sketches, charts and plans of curricular or local interest are among the materials generally considered ephemeral.

Ephemeral materials should be organized economically with a minimum of cataloguing yet in a manner which will ensure their easy retrieval. This can be effected by placing these materials in a vertical file and indexing them by one of the following methods:

1. For a particular item, the appropriate heading is selected from the subject heading list used for other media centre materials. The item is placed in a file folder labelled with this subject heading, and the folder is filed alphabetically in the vertical file. Directions for the retrieval of items are filed under the appropriate heading in the catalogue. The following guide card is suggested:

Sample card 123

2. For a particular item, the appropriate classification number is selected from the classification scheme used for other media centre materials. The item is placed in a file folder labelled with this number, and the folder is filed numerically in the vertical file. Directions for the retrieval of items are filed under the appropriate heading in the card catalogue. The following guide card is suggested:

Sample card 124

VOLCANOES

Additional material on this subject will be found in the vertical file under 551.21.

Items of permanent value to the collection should be completely catalogued for their effective use. However, if a media centre has a small staff with limited time to devote to cataloguing, some media, e.g., picture sets, study prints, transparencies, single slides, art prints, maps, can be organized informally. The following guide card is suggested for filing in the catalogue:

Sample card 125

VOLCANOES

Additional material on the above subject will be found in the special collections indicated below

☐ Vertical file   ☐ Slide trays

☐ Map drawer   ☐ Art collection

☐ Picture file   ☐

References to In-depth Indexing

Many media centres have various indexes and lists to supplement the main catalogue. These specialized lists, often computer produced, include analytics and other in-depth indexing in certain subject fields. The public catalogue should direct the patron's attention to the existence of such lists. The following guide cards are suggested:

Beethoven, Ludwig van.

SEE ALSO Audiodisc Catalogue at Information Desk for
other recordings of works by this composer.

PANCREAS

Additional information on this subject will be found by
consulting special lists in the departments indicated below

☐ Government Publications Division

☐ Medical Division Library

☐ Serials Division

☐ Science Division

Glossary and Abbreviations 4

Glossary

The definitions in this glossary have been constructed for descriptive cataloguing purposes only. Definitive technical descriptions have not been attempted. Media designations are indicated in bold face.

Aperture card *see* **Microform**

Art original *see* **Diorama; Model; Picture; Realia**

Art print *see* **Picture**

Art reproduction *see* **Diorama; Model; Picture**

Artifact *see* **Realia**

Audiodisc *see* **Audiorecord**

Audiocylinder *see* **Audiorecord**

Audiorecord[1] – A recording of sound in one of the following formats: cylinder, disc, roll, magnetic tape, wire.

Audioroll *see* **Audiorecord**

Audiotape *see* **Audiorecord**

Audiowire *see* **Audiorecord**

Cartridge – an enclosed container for film or magnetic tape in an endless loop format.

Cassette – An enclosed container for film or magnetic tape in reel-to-reel format.

Chart – A sheet of information arranged in tabular or graphic form. Includes the following format: *Flip chart* – An integrated graphic presentation on separate sheets hinged together, designed to be used on an easel.

Collation – A term used in descriptive cataloguing to describe the physical characteristics of an item.

Diorama – A three-dimensional scale model of a scene created by placing objects and figures in front of a representational background.

Electronic video recording *see* **Videorecord**

Filmslip *see* **Filmstrip**

Filmstrip – A roll of film, usually 16 mm. or 35 mm., containing a succession of images designed to be viewed frame by frame, with or without sound. Includes the following format: *Filmslip* – A short length of film containing a succession of images designed to be viewed frame by frame, sometimes mounted in a rigid format.

Flash card – A card printed with words, numerals, or pictures, designed for rapid identification, with or without sound.

Flip chart *see* **Chart**

Game – A set of materials, usually boxed, designed for play or competition.

Globe – A sphere with a representation or a map of the earth or the universe. Includes the following format: *Relief globe* – A globe which indicates different heights of land forms by means of a raised surface.

Graph *see* **Chart**

Hologram – A method of producing images using a laser beam. Medium designation used: **Motion Picture; Videorecord,** etc.

Imprint – A term used in descriptive cataloguing to represent place of publication, name of publisher or producer, and date.

Kit – Two or more media which are not fully interdependent and, therefore, may be used separately.

Laboratory kit – Boxed co-ordinated materials designed to promote specific learning experiences. Medium designations used: **Game; Kit,** etc.

Logical record – A single unit of information consisting of one or more fields or variables.

Machine readable data file – Information coded by methods that require the use of a machine (typically but not always a computer) for translation. Includes the following formats: disc pack, magnetic tape, mark-sensed cards, optical character recognition font documents, punched cards with or without magnetic tape strip, punched paper tape, etc.

Map – A flat representation of part or all of either the earth or the universe. Includes the following format: *Relief map* – A map which indicates different heights of land forms by means of a raised surface.

Microfiche *see* **Microform**

Microfilm *see* **Microform**

Microform – A miniature of printed or other graphic matter which cannot be utilized without magnification. Includes the following formats:

Aperture card – A card with an opening or openings within which a microform on film is mounted.

Microfiche – A microform on a flat sheet of film.

Microfilm – A microform on a roll of film.

Micro-opaque – A microform on opaque material.

Microscope slide – A specialized slide produced specifically for use with a microscope.

Mock-up *see* **Model**

Model – A three-dimensional representation of

---

[1] See footnote on page 7.

a real object, either exact or to scale; a mock-up.

Motion picture – Film, with or without sound track, bearing a sequence of images which create the illusion of movement when projected. Includes the following format: *Motion picture loop* – An endless loop of motion picture film usually contained in a cartridge.

Motion picture loop *see* **Motion Picture**

Phonocylinder *see* **Audiorecord**

Phonodisc *see* **Audiorecord**

Phonorecord *see* **Audiorecord**

Phonoroll *see* **Audiorecord**

Phonotape *see* **Audiorecord**

Phonowire *see* **Audiorecord**

Picture – A two-dimensional drawing, painting, photograph, portrait, or print of any of these, produced on an opaque backing. Includes the following formats:
Art original – A work of art, e.g., painting, drawing, etc.
Art print – A printed reproduction of a work of art.
Photograph – An image produced on a photo-sensitized surface by a camera.
Post card – A card for bearing a message through the mail without an envelope.
Poster – A bill or placard intended to be posted.
Study print – A picture with accompanying text which makes the print significant for study purposes.

Photograph *see* **Picture**

Post card *see* **Picture**

Poster *see* **Picture**

Programmed instruction – An educational technique designed for self-instruction and testing, utilizing the sequencing of information into basic logical units, and providing the learner with knowledge of results.

Realia – Actual objects; artifacts, samples, specimens.

Relief map *see* **Map**

Sample *see* **Realia**

Slide – A small unit of transparent material, usually 2 x 2 in., 2¼ x 2¼ in., or 3¼ x 4 in., in rigid format and designed for use in a slide viewer or projector. Includes the following format: *Stereograph* – Slides presented in pairs, designed to produce a three-dimensional effect when used with a stereoscope viewer or projector.

Specimen *see* **Realia**

Stereograph *see* **Slide**

Stereoscopic slide *see* **Slide**

Study print *see* **Picture**

Transparency – An image produced on transparent material, usually 8½ x 10 in., designed for use with an overhead projector.

Uniform title – The particular title by which a work that has appeared under varying titles is to be identified for cataloguing purposes.

Videocassette *see* **Videorecord**

Videodisc *see* **Videorecord**

Videorecord – A recording designed for television playback. Includes the following formats:
Electronic video recording (trade name) – A videorecord on 8.75 mm. film.
Videocassette – A videorecord on magnetic tape, enclosed in a cassette.
Videodisc – A videorecord on a disc.
Videotape – A videorecord on magnetic tape.

Videotape *see* **Videorecord**

Abbreviations

b&w	black and white	n.d.	no date
col.	colour	photo(s).	photograph(s)
fr.	frames	quadra.	quadraphonic
in.	inches	rpm.	revolutions per minute
ips.	inches per second	s.	side
l.	leaves	sd.	sound
mm.	millimetres	si.	silent
min.	minutes	stereo.	stereophonic
mono.	monaural		

Storage 5

General Suggestions for the Storage of an Integrated Collection

It is impossible to predict future developments in the rapidly changing media field. Storage requirements vary for each media centre and no single storage system is applicable to all. Manufacturers will continue to develop new equipment in response to media centres' needs.

The following guidelines apply to an integrated media centre, i.e., one which uses a single subject analysis system for all media and maintains an omnimedia catalogue.
1. All circulating materials are stored together in one room or complex of rooms. Nonbook materials should not be relegated to a room accessible only to the staff of the media centre.
2. Open display storage is used for all materials, wherever possible. Storage in drawers and cabinets should be reduced to a minimum.
3. Rigid partitioning should be avoided. Flexible storage provides ease in interfiling classified items.
4. When media must be stored in containers, transparent materials are recommended for packaging. For instance, realia can be stored in clear plastic boxes.

Enclosed and inconvenient storage involves an uneconomical use of staff time and an unnecessary delay in service.

Total intershelving
Intershelving of all materials is the ideal arrangement for collections which may be browsed by the public. It results in more frequent, more effective use of all materials by bringing to the patrons' attention the interrelationship of media.

It should be noted that because of rapid developments in packaging, media which are now considered to be unsuited to browsing may not be so regarded in future.

Partial intershelving
Because of the wide range in shapes and sizes of media, intershelving may consume more space than specialized shelving for each medium. For media centres which do not have sufficient storage space to allow total intershelving, the following suggestions for partial intershelving are offered:
1. Individual multi-media shelves which can be placed throughout the regular book shelves are available commercially. These shelves enable the media centre to locate all the nonbook materials on a given subject together on one or two shelves contiguous to books on the same subject.
2. Book trucks can be fitted to house nonbook materials, so that nonbook materials in a given subject area may be placed near the book shelves containing the same subject.

Segregated shelving
Archival collections must be kept in conditions best suited to the preservation of a particular medium. Intershelving may then be a lesser consideration. Any media centre which does not provide direct public access to its collection may not need to intershelve its material.

If a media centre's collection is not intershelved, or if part of its collection is held in other buildings, the entries for all its materials should still be interfiled in one catalogue in an area readily accessible to the public. In addition to this omnimedia catalogue, individual collections in other buildings or areas may have their own catalogues.

GENERAL GUIDELINES FOR THE CARE, HANDLING, AND STORAGE OF AUDIODISCS

Care
Discs must be kept free of dust and dirt. Distilled water applied with a lint-free cloth is the most economical and efficient method of cleaning discs.

Stereophonic and quadraphonic grooves are easily damaged by heavy tone arms, improper anti-skate adjustment, or styli which are worn or the wrong size. Media centre playback equipment must be maintained by qualified personnel.

Handling
Discs should be handled as little as possible and then only by the edges.

Storage
Temperature: discs should be kept at a stable temperature of about 70 degrees F. Excessive heat (especially direct sunlight) will cause them to warp within a matter of hours.

Humidity: discs will attract dust when humidity is low enough to cause a build-up of static electricity.

Shelving: discs should never be stored so that they are supporting the weight of other discs. They should be shelved standing on edge, spine out, if they are not used frequently. For short term storage in a rapidly circulating collection, browser bins allow maximum access with minimum damage.

Intershelving of audiodiscs with other materials is facilitated by individual bins attached to book shelving. These bins, which are available commercially, may be pulled out for browsing convenience.

GENERAL GUIDELINES FOR THE CARE, HANDLING, AND STORAGE OF FILM MEDIA
(Filmstrips, Microforms, Motion Pictures, Slides, Transparencies)

Care
Film should be cleaned and inspected after each use. Infrequently used film should be inspected regularly.

Film transport and optical equipment must be kept clean and dust-free.

Only qualified staff should attempt to repair either equipment or film.

Handling
Film must be kept away from sources of dust and objects which can scratch or tear it.

Film should not be jarred or dropped. Such treatment may produce cinch marks (short scratches) throughout the length of the film. Bent containers or reels can damage film severely.

Film should be handled only by the edges and should not be twisted.

Film must never get wet.

Film should be allowed to reach room temperature before it is screened.

Projection equipment and viewers must be mounted safely and all power cords secured.

The operator must not leave the machine while motion pictures are being projected or rewound. At the first sign of trouble, the projector must be stopped and rethreaded if necessary. If film *must* be re-fastened, *only* tape which will not remove the emulsion should be used.

Storage
Temperature: film must not be stored in direct sunlight or near sources of heat. It should not be subjected to temperature changes of more than 20 degrees F. 70 degrees F. is optimum storage temperature, but extremes of 60 degrees F. and 90 degrees F. are tolerable.

Humidity: 50% relative humidity provides the ideal storage environment for film. The normal humidity range in a media centre is tolerable. Polyester film will not dry out as quickly as other types.

Container: film should be stored in dust-proof containers. These should be carefully selected to ensure that they are not composed of materials harmful to film, such as acid, sulphur, or peroxide.

Film stored on reels should be secured with a tape which will not remove the emulsion, e.g., masking tape. Rubber bands must not be used unless they have been specially manufactured without sulphur, and are loose enough to allow for expansion and contraction without cinching the film.

GENERAL GUIDELINES FOR THE CARE, HANDLING, AND STORAGE OF MAGNETIC TAPES
(Audiotapes, Sound Tracks of Various Media, Videotapes)

Care
In archival collections a tape which has not been used for a year should be rewound.

Handling
The tape itself should be touched as little as possible.

Storage
Temperature and Humidity: extremes in the storage area should be avoided. Temperature may range from 40 degrees F. to 80 degrees F., relative humidity from 30% to 60%. Ideal conditions for archival storage are 70 degrees F. and 50% relative humidity.

Container and Shelving: magnetic tapes should be stored in dust-proof containers, standing on edge, with proper supports to prevent their falling.

The storage area and/or shelving must not be subject to vibrations and must be free of all magnetic fields.

GENERAL GUIDELINES FOR THE CARE, HANDLING, AND STORAGE OF MICROSCOPE SLIDES

Microscope slides can withstand normal media centre usage and storage conditions, if during their construction the mounting medium has been allowed to dry properly. Slides should not be stored in direct sunlight, which might crack or melt resins and fade stains.

Ideal conditions for collections of valuable slides would include, in addition to the above, storage in areas of cool temperatures (60 to 65 degrees F.) and low humidity.

GENERAL GUIDELINES FOR THE STORAGE OF THREE-DIMENSIONAL MATERIALS
(Games, Globes, Kits, Models, Realia)

Because of diversity in shape and composition, no general guidelines have been included for the care and handling of three-dimensional materials.

Wherever possible three-dimensional materials should be shelved with or near other media in the same subject field. The storage container should be as descriptive as possible of its contents. If the producer's container is colourful, descriptive, durable, and not over-large in comparison to its contents, intershelve in this container. If, however, the producer's container does not conform to at least two of these requirements or if the item has been acquired without a suitable container, materials should be stored in transparent containers which will allow the media centre user to browse the collection. Alternatively, any type of container may be used if it is labelled with a description, and possibly a picture, of the contents. Adequate labelling will allow browsing of opaque containers.

GENERAL GUIDELINES FOR THE CARE, HANDLING, AND STORAGE OF TWO-DIMENSIONAL, OPAQUE MATERIALS
(Charts, Flash Cards, Maps, Pictures)

Time and money should not be spent on the care of uncatalogued, ephemeral materials. The following guidelines apply to catalogued media which are part of a permanent collection.

Many books and pamphlets have been written about the care and storage of art prints, pictures, photographs, etc. Media centres with valuable materials should consult authoritative texts for advice about their preservation. These books should also be read for a fuller discussion of points listed below.

These brief guidelines apply to items in a permanent collection which are not very val-

uable or rare and which circulate with other media centre materials.

1. Some recommended methods to make fragile materials more durable are indicated below:
   Edging. The life of a map, picture, or similar material will be lengthened if it is edged with acetate fibre. Manual edging machines are available commercially.
   Lamination. Laminating equipment is now used by media centres for many purposes, e.g., covering book jackets.
   Mounting. The mounting materials must be acid-free.
   Spraying. Clear acrylic may be sprayed on the surface of pictures to protect them from finger marks, dirt, etc.
   Vinyl picture covers. These are useful for circulating fragile two-dimensional materials.

2. Dirt and grease from fingers and other sources can damage two-dimensional, opaque materials. Therefore, they should be stored in envelopes made of acid-free materials.

3. It is unwise to use most pressure sensitive tapes because they will discolour paper with a stain which is impossible to remove.

4. Newspaper clippings can be kept in their original form if they are backed with 100% rag mounting and stored in folders made of acid-free paper.

5. Photographs are particularly vulnerable to careless handling.
   a) Rubber cement or other rubber compounds, gummed or plastic tape can damage photographs. Dry mounting tissue should be used.
   b) Excessive heat and humidity should be avoided. (Negatives should be stored in metal, polyethylene, or styrene because wood and cardboard absorb moisture)
   c) Dirt, dust, light, and finger marks can cause deterioration. Photographs should be stored individually in seamless cellulose acetate envelopes or seamless all-rag envelopes.
   d) Writing on the back of photographs produces undesirable ridges on the face of the picture. Descriptive material should be typed on a separate sheet and placed in the envelope with the photograph.

Storage of Two-Dimensional Materials (including Transparencies)
Many two-dimensional materials are produced in containers suitable for intershelving. These include sets of transparencies in boxes or binders and similar materials. Single items of slight depth easily overlooked by the media centre

patron should be shelved in brightly coloured envelopes.

Some two-dimensional materials need additional treatment before they can be intershelved. Maps with covers shelve easily; only the folds need reinforcing to prolong life. Where surface creases are tolerable, flat materials, such as charts and maps, should be folded rather than rolled, and the folds reinforced with suitable material. These folded items may then be placed in a manilla envelope, transparent bag, or box and intershelved with the rest of the collection.

A large collection of maps or other flat materials, which is not intershelved with other media, and unmounted materials which must be preserved uncreased should be filed flat where possible, and stored in waist-high horizontal map cases. This type of storage enables items to be consulted on top of the cases and minimizes handling.

Large-sized, mounted materials should be housed on open display devices. Such storage is being produced by many manufacturers in response to the current fad for posters.

Appendices 6

Alternative Method of Cataloguing a Specialized, Non-Integrated Collection of Maps[1]

Appendix A

There appears to be no completely satisfactory method of cataloguing maps for an omnimedia catalogue. The *Anglo-American Cataloging Rules* produces too many entries under publisher, e.g., Rand McNally Co., resulting in catalogue drawers full of cards with the same not-too-useful main entry. Title main entry is useful for maps with distinctive titles, but many maps have non-distinctive titles or no titles.

Entry under geographic area is preferred by many map librarians, but this method of entry makes very difficult the interfiling of these cards with those of other media.

The following rules of entry have been suggested by several map librarians for large collections of maps which will *not* be integrated into an omnimedia catalogue.

Main entry

Maps are entered under the name of the area covered, subdivided by the predominant subject matter illustrated, with a further subdivision for the date of the situation depicted, e.g., [U.S. – National parks and reserves – 1971]. This supplied main entry is enclosed in square brackets.

Maps with no predominant subject matter are entered under area subdivided by date, e.g., [Ontario – 1930].

If date is implicit in the main entry for historical maps, it may be omitted.

Establishing Supplied Main Entry for Maps and Geographic Models

Specific geographic names must be selected from standard and authoritative lists. Subject subdivisions should follow as closely as possible the wording of the subject heading list used.

The following bibliography is a suggested list of sources for geographic names. It is not meant to be exhaustive.

American Geographical Society of New York. *Cataloging and filing rules for maps and atlases in the Society's collection,* by Roman Drazniowsky. Rev. and expanded ed. New York, 1969. (Its mimeographed and offset publication, no. 4) (This publication provides lists of geographic names and subject subdivisions.)

The Columbia Lippincott gazeteer of the world, edited by Leon E. Seltzer . . . New York, Columbia University Press, 1962

The Times, London. *Index-gazeteer of the world.* London, Times Publishing Co., 1965

U.S. Board on Geographic Names. *Gazeteers.* Washington, Government Printing Office, 1955- (The most complete reference is provided in this set comprised of over 120 volumes. Its large size makes it impractical for a small collection.)

U.S. Department of State. Office of the Geographer. *Geographic bulletins.* Washington, Government Printing Office, 1965- (These Bulletins are useful for information about new countries and name changes.)

Media centres which have a small collection of geographic nonbook materials may find satisfactory geographic names listed in *Webster's Geographical Dictionary.*

Small collections may be organized also by using standard subject heading lists (e.g., Sears or Library of Congress) for establishing supplied geographic main entries. Subject headings which begin with a geographic name are selected easily from these lists. Useful subject headings, which are subdivided geographically, can be reversed for supplied entry use, e.g., "National parks and reserves – U.S." listed in Sears may be changed to [U.S. – National parks and reserves]. This applies only to a supplied geographic main entry. Such a reversal cannot be used in a tracing or subject added entry.

The class numbers used on sample cards 128 and 129 are from Boggs and Lewis' special map classification.[2]

---

[1] This appendix has been included at the request of several map librarians. We are indebted to Miss Joan Winearls, Map Librarian, University of Toronto, for her helpful assistance.

[2] Boggs, Samuel W. and Dorothy Cornwell Lewis. *The classification and cataloging of maps and alases.* New York, Special Libraries Association, 1945.

Sample card 128

```
676          [Wisconsin.  1967]
1968S            State of Wisconsin.  U.S. Geological Survey, 1968.
                 1 map.  col.  112 x 107 cm.


                 1:500,000.
                 Lambert conformal conic projection.
                 Relief contours.




                 1. Wisconsin.  I. U.S.  Geological Survey.
```

Sample card 129

```
610          [Canada.  Eskimos.  1964]
1964D            Distribution of Eskimo population.   Repartition de la population
             Esquimaude.  Water Resources Branch, Dept. of Northern Affairs
             and National Resources  [196-?]
                 1 map (printed both sides)  b&w.  18 x 23 cm.


                 1:20,000,000.
                 English edition 1 side,  French edition other side.



                 1. Eskimos - Canada.  I. Canada.  Water Resources Branch.
             II. Title.
```

International Standard Bibliographic Description

The *International Standard Bibliographic Description (for Single Volume and Multi-Volume Monographic Publications)* published in 1971 by the International Federation of Library Associations Committee on Cataloguing has been adopted by several national bibliographies, and will be the basis for a revision of Chapter 6 of the *Anglo-American Cataloging Rules.* The foreword of the document states:

"It is designed primarily as an instrument for the international communication of bibliographical information. By specifying the elements which should comprise a bibliographical description and by prescribing the order in which they should be presented and the punctuation by which they should be demarcated, it aims at three objectives: to make records from different sources interchangeable; to facilitate their interpretation across language barriers; and to facilitate the conversion of such records to machine-readable form."

While the ISBD has been designed for book cataloguing, its principles can, and undoubtedly will, be extended to nonbook cataloguing. Libraries planning to adopt ISBD should apply its format to all materials.

Sample cards 130 and 131 suggest the way in which ISBD might be applied to nonbook cataloguing.

Sample card 130

```
759        Realism, man's environment   (Filmstrip).  -  Visual Publications,
REA           c1970.
              31 double fr.:   col.;   35 mm. -  (Art appreciation;  11)

           Manual (7 p.) compiled and annotated by Anthony Bertram.
           Series title on manual:   Appreciation  of pictures.




              1. Realism in art.   I. Series.   II. Series:  Appreciation of pictures.
```

Filmstrip.

Sample card 131

```
LB         Scott, Ralph, 1927-
1513          Classification and seriation kit   (Kit)/Ralph Scott, Ned Ratekin
           [and] Kay F. Kramer. - Harper & Row, 1968.
              blocks in box, 7 envelopes with markers and cards, 1 guidebook
           (270 p.), mask, 19 transparencies in binder. - (The Learning readiness
           system)




              1. Learning by discovery.  2. Education, Primary.  I. Ratekin,
           Ned.  II. Kramer, Kay F.  III. Title.  IV. Series.
```

Kit.

Bibliography

American Library Association. Public Library Association. Audiovisual Committee. *Guidelines for audiovisual materials & services for public libraries.* Chicago, Ill., 1970

Anglo-American cataloging rules; North American text, ed. by C. Sumner Spalding. Chicago: American Library Association, 1967

Anglo-American cataloguing rules; British text, ed. by C. Sumner Spalding. London: The Library Association, 1967

Association for Educational Communications and Technology. Information Science Committee. *Standards for cataloging nonprint materials.* 3d ed. Washington, D.C., 1972

Badten, Jean and Nancy Motomatzu. "Commercial media cataloging – what's holding us up?" *School Library Journal,* 15, no. 3 (November 1968) pp. 34-35

Berger, Ivan. "Tape today: reel-to-reel, cartridge, or cassette?" *Saturday Review,* 52 (September 27, 1969) pp. 49-55

Bissell, Leah and Arthur Hoisington. *Cataloging guide for non-book materials.* Auburn, Wash.: Auburn School District no. 408, n.d.

Boggs, S. W. and D. C. Lewis. *The classification and cataloging of maps and atlases.* New York: Special Libraries Association, 1945

Bretz, Rudy. *A taxonomy of communication media.* Englewood Cliffs, N.J.: Educational Technology Publications, 1971

Bryant, E. T. *Music librarianship; a practical guide.* London: Clarke, 1959

Burkett, J. and T. S. Morgan, eds. *Special materials in the library.* London: The Library Association, 1963

Canadian Library Association. Technical Services Section. *A list of Canadian subject headings.* Edited by Joan Mitchell, Hazel I. McTaggart, and Nicholas Krenta, for the Technical Services Section of the Canadian Library Association. Ottawa, 1968

Chibnall, Bernard and Antony Croghan. *A feasibility study of a multi-media catalogue; report to the Office for Scientific and Technical Information.* [Brighton] University of Sussex, 1969

Clugston, Katharine W. "Anglo-American cataloging rules: film cataloging at the Library of Congress." *Library Resources & Technical Services,* 13, no. 1 (Winter 1969) pp. 35-41

College of DuPage. Instructional Resources Center. *Processing manual for books and non-book materials.* Glen Ellyn, Ill., 1968

Colvin, Laura C. *Cataloging sampler; a comparative and interpretive guide.* Hamden, Conn.: Archon, 1963

"Commercial media cataloging – what's around?" *School Library Journal,* 15, no. 3 (November 1968) pp. 27-33

Croghan, Antony. *A thesaurus-classification for non-book media.* London, the author, 1970

Cunha, George Daniel Martin. *Conservation of library materials; a manual and bibliography on the care, repair and restoration of library materials.* Metuchen, N.J.: Scarecrow Press, 1967

Currall, Henry F. J., ed. *Gramaphone record libraries: their organization and practice.* 2d ed. London: Crosley Lockwood, 1970 (New librarianship series)

Daily, Jay E. "The selection, processing, and storage of non-print materials: a critique of the Anglo-American Cataloging rules as they relate to the newer media." *Library Trends,* 16, no. 2 (October 1967) pp. 283-89

Design for cataloging non-book materials: adaptable to computer use. Rochester, N.Y.: The Genesee Valley School Development Association, c1969

Dewey, Melvil. *Abridged Dewey decimal classification and relative index.* Ed. 10. Lake Placid Club, N.Y.: Forest Press of Lake Placid Club Education Foundation, 1971

Dewey, Melvil. *Dewey decimal classification and relative index.* 3 v. Ed. 18. Lake Placid Club, N.Y.: Forest Press of Lake Placid Club Education Foundation, 1971

Egan, Mary J. "Tiptoe in technology." *School Library Journal,* 13, no. 8 (April 1967) pp. 49-51

Elrod, J. McRee and John McKinley. *Cataloguing and classification of non-book materials (audiovisual, microform, and manuscript) in the University of British Columbia library system.* Vancouver, B.C., 1970

Gaver, Mary V., ed. *The elementary school library collection.* Phases 1-2-3. 6th ed. Newark, N.J.: Bro-Dart Foundation, 1971

Gerletti, Robert C. "Digital apoplexy: certain diagnosis, no easy cure." *School Library Journal,* 15, no. 3 (November 1968) pp. 36-37

Grove, Pearce S. and Evelyn G. Clement, eds. *Bibliographic control of nonprint media.* Chicago, Ill.: American Library Association, 1972

Hall, David. "Phonorecord preservation; notes of a pragmatist." *Special Libraries*, 62, no. 9 (September 1971) pp. 357-362

Harris, Evelyn J. *Instructional materials cataloging guide*. Tucson, Ariz.: University of Arizona College of Education, Bureau of Educational Research, 1968

Harrod, Leonard Montague. *The librarians' glossary of terms used in librarianship and the book crafts, and reference book*. 3d rev. ed. New York: Seminar Press, 1971. (Grafton library science series)

Hawken, William R. *Copying methods manual*. Chicago, Ill.: Library Technology Program, American Library Association, 1966. (LTP publications, 11)

Hicks, Warren B. and Alma M. Tillin. *Developing multi-media libraries*. New York: R. R. Bowker, 1970

Hoffberg, Judith A. "To preserve and to protect: a call to action." *Picturescope*, v. 19, no. 2 (Summer 1971) pp. 84-90

International Association of Music Libraries. *Phonograph record libraries, their organization and practice*. Ed. by H. F. J. Currall and A. H. King. Hamden, Conn.: Archon, 1963

Ireland, Norma Olin. *The picture file in school, college, and public libraries*. Rev. & enl. ed. Boston, Mass.: Faxon, 1952

Johnson, Jean Thornton and others. *AV cataloging and processing simplified*. Raleigh, N.C.: Audiovisual Catalogers, 1971

Koelling, Robert B. "Integrated multi-media shelving works." *Audiovisual Instruction*, 17, no. 7 (September 1972) pp. 50

Kujoth, Jean Spealman, ed. *Readings in nonbook librarianship*. Metuchen, N.J.: Scarecrow Press, 1968

Landau, Thomas, ed. *Encyclopaedia of librarianship*. 3d rev. ed. London: Bowes, 1966

Laurenta, Sister Mary. "Classifying and cataloging filmstrips, records and tapes." *Catholic Library World*, 38, no. 4 (December 1966) pp. 242-43

Lembo, Diana. "A stepchild comes of age." *School Library Journal*, 14, no. 1 (September 1967) pp. 54-55

Loertscher, David V. *Manual for cataloging non-book materials*. Bellevue Public Schools, 1968

Lubetzky, Seymour. *Principles of cataloging*. Los Angeles, Calif.: Institute of Library Research, University of California, 1969

March, Ivan. *Running a record library*. Blackpool, Eng.: Long Playing Record Library, 1965

Meerdink, Richard E. "The control of nonbook materials: an alternative approach." *The Southeastern Librarian*, 19, no. 3 (Fall 1971) pp. 176-78

"'Microbooks' a new library medium?" *Publishers' Weekly*, 198 (November 9, 1970) pp. 48-50

Miller, Shirley. *The vertical file and its satellites; a handbook of acquisition, processing and organization*. Littleton, Colo.: Libraries Unlimited, 1971. (Library science text series)

Moriarty, John H. "New media facilities." *Library Trends*, 16, no. 2 (October 1967) pp. 251-258

Music Library Association. *Manual of music librarianship*. Ed. by Carol June Bradley. [n.p.] 1966

Myers, Nat C. "The story of 8 mm cartridges." *Educational Screen and Audiovisual Guide*, 49, no. 9 (September 1969) pp. 10-11, 15

National Education Association. Dept. of Audiovisual Instruction. *Standards for cataloging, coding and scheduling educational media*. Washington, D.C., 1968

Natonal Medical Audiovisual Center. Reference and Archival Section. *Cataloging nonprint at NMAC; a guide for the medical librarian*. [Washington, D.C.] Department of Health, Education, and Welfare, 1971

National Microfilm Association. *Glossary of micrographics*. Silver Spring, Md., 1971. (NMA Standard MS-100-1971)

Nelson, Carl E. *Microfilm technology: engineering and related fields*. New York: McGraw-Hill, 1965

Nitecki, Joseph Z. "Simplified classification and cataloging of microfroms." *Library Resources & Technical Services*, 13, no. 1 (Winter 1969) pp. 79-85

North Carolina. State Dept. of Public Instruction. Division of Educational Media. *Organizing audiovisual materials in the school media collection*. Raleigh, N.C., 1970

Ontario Dept. of Education. *The library handbook for elementary schools in Ontario*. Toronto, 1967

Parkhurst, Perrin E. "A comparative analysis of three new TV storage systems; Electronic Video Recording, Selectavision, cassette videotape recording." *Audiovisual Instruction*, 15, no. 9 (November 1970) pp. 43-50

Pearson, Mary D. *Recordings in the public library*. Chicago, Ill.: American Library Association, 1963

Piercy, Esther J. *Commonsense cataloging*. New York: H. W. Wilson, 1965

Plunkett, Dalton G. and Allan D. Quick. *Cataloging standards for non-book materials; a complete guide to cataloging non-book materials in the individual school*. Tizard, Ore.: Northwest Library Service, 1968

Pressler, Joan. "Organizing library-based A-V materials." *School Libraries*, 14, no. 3 (March 1965) pp. 43-47

Prostano, Emanuel T. *School media programs:*

case studies in management. Metuchen, N.J.: Scarecrow Press, 1970

Rawkins, Reginald A. "Don Mills uses Dewey to classify pamphlets." *Ontario Library Review,* 50, no. 1 (February 1966) pp. 14-15

Redfern, Brian. *Organizing music in libraries.* London: Bingley, 1966

Reichmann, Felix and Josephine M. Tharpe. *Determination of an effective system of bibliographic control of microform publications.* Washington, D.C.: Association of Research Libraries, 1970

Ristow, Walter W. and David K. Carrington. "Machine-readable map cataloging in the Library of Congress." *Special Libraries,* 62, no. 9 (September 1971) pp. 343-352

Robbins, Donald C. "Current resources for the bibliographic control of sound recordings." *Library Trends,* 21, no. 1 (July 1972) pp. 136-46

Rufsvold, Margaret I. and Carolyn Guss. *Guides to newer educational media.* 3d ed. Chicago, Ill.: American Library Association, 1971

Saheb-Ettaba, Caroline and Roger B. Mc-Farlane. *ANSCR; the alpha-numeric system for classification of recordings . . . .* Williamsport, Penn.: Bro-Dart, 1969

Sanderson, Jessie Mae. *Non-book library materials, a cataloging guide.* Livonia, Mich.: Livonia Public Schools. Dept. of Instructional Materials Services, 1965

Scholz, Dell Dubose. *A manual for the cataloging of recordings in public libraries.* Rev. ed. Baton Rouge, La.: Louisiana Library Association, 1964

Scott, Margaret B. and Doris P. Fennell. *Cataloguing for school libraries; a guide to simplified form.* 2d ed. Toronto: Pergamon of Canada, 1970

Sears, Minnie Earl. *List of subject headings.* 10th ed. by Barbara M. Westby. New York: H. W. Wilson Company, 1972

Simonton, Wesley. "The bibliographical control of microforms." *Library Resources & Technical Services,* 6, no. 1 (Winter 1962) pp. 29-40

Smith, Thomas R. *The map collection in a general library; a manual for classification and processing procedures.* Lawrence, Kan.: University of Kansas, 1961

Snow, Kathleen M. *Manual for cataloguing non-book materials.* Calgary, Alta.: University of Calgary Bookstore, 1968

Steele, Robert. *The cataloging and classification of cinema literature.* Metuchen, N.J.: Scarecrow Press, 1967

Stoops, Betty. "Cataloging and classification systems for instructional materials." *Audiovisual Instruction,* 9, no. 7 (September 1964) pp. 427-28

Sunder, Mary Jane. "Organization of recorded sound." *Library Resources & Technical Services,* 13, no. 1 (Winter 1969) pp. 93-98

Taylor, Virginia. *Non-print materials: cataloging and processing.* Houston, Texas: Instructional Materials Services, Houston Independent School District, 1970

Tebbel, John. "Libraries in miniature: a new era begins." *Saturday Review,* 54 (January 9, 1971) pp. 41-42

U.S. Library of Congress. Information Systems Office. *Maps, a MARC format; specifications for magnetic tapes containing catalog records for maps.* Washington, D.C., 1970

U.S. Library of Congress. MARC Development Office. *Films, a MARC format; specifications for magnetic tapes containing catalog records for motion pictures, filmstrips, and other pictorial media intended for projection.* Washington, D.C., 1970

U.S. Library of Congress. Subject Cataloging Division. *Music subject headings used on printed catalog cards of the Library of Congress.* Washington, D.C., 1952

U.S. Library of Congress. Subject Cataloging Division. *Subject headings used in the dictionary catalogs of the Library of Congress.* 7th ed. by Marguerite V. Quattlebaum. Washington, D.C., 1966

Veaner, Allen B. *The evaluation of micropublications; a handbook for librarians.* Chicago, Ill.: Library Technology Program, American Library Association, 1971. (LTP publications, 17)

Veit, Fritz. "Microforms, microform equipment and microform use in the educational environment." *Library Trends,* 19, no. 4 (April 1971) pp. 447-466

Watts, Cecil E. *How to clean, maintain and protect records; their nature, mechanics, maintenance.* New Hyde Park, N.Y.: Elpa Marketing Industries, n.d.

Waygood, A. "Hints on storing non-print materials." *Index* 1, no. 1 (Spring 1968) pp. 24-25

Waygood, A. "Welcome to the school library." *Ontario Library Review,* 51, no. 4 (December 1967) pp. 218-21

Welch, Walter L. "Preservation and restoration of authenticity in sound recordings." *Library Trends,* 21, no. 1 (July 1972) pp. 83-100

Western Michigan University. Dept. of Librarianship. *Manual for processing non-book materials in school libraries, for use in course 531: Technical processes.* Rev. Kalamazoo, 1966

Westhuis, Judith Loveys and Julia M. DeYoung. *Cataloging manual for non-book materials in learning centers and school libraries*. Rev. ed. Ann Arbor, Mich.: Michigan Association of School Librarians, 1967

Winnipeg School Division no. 1. Library Service Centre. *Manual for cataloguing and storage of non-book materials*. Winnipeg, Man., 1967

Winston, Fred and Mildred Winston. "Indexing and cataloging the 8 mm." *The Instructor,* 78, no. 5 (January 1969)

Wynar, Bohdan S. *Introduction to cataloging and classification*. 4th ed. Rochester, N.Y.: Libraries Unlimited, 1971. (Library science text series)

Yesner, Bernice L. *Administering filmstrip and record collections*. n.p. McGraw, 1968

Zaccarian, P. and C. B. B. Wood. *Video player and recorder systems for home use*. Brussels: European Broadcasting Union Technical Centre, 1971. (Tech. 3093-E)

Index